How to Write
and Market a
Christmas
Cozy Mystery

T. LOCKHAVEN

EDITED BY

GRACE LOCKHAVEN

TWISTED KEY
p u b l i s h i n g

2021

ISBN 978-1-63911-028-5

Twisted Key Publishing, LLC
www.twistedkeypublishing.com

Ordering Information:
Special discounts are available on quantity purchases by corporations, associations, educators, and others. For details, contact the publisher at the above listed address.

U.S. trade bookstores and wholesalers: Please contact Twisted Key Publishing, LLC by email twistedkeypublishing@gmail.com.

To Emily Pearl, who made every Christmas magical.
You are dearly missed.

Table of Contents

Introduction 1

Chapter 1 Christmas Cozy Mystery Writing 3

Rules and Expectations 4

What Readers *Want* from a Christmas Mystery 10

Exercise 12

What Readers *Don't* want from a Christmas Mystery 15

The death knell 23

Chapter 2 Amateur Sleuth 24

A few examples of famous Sleuths 25

Creating Your Amateur Sleuth 29

Basics 31

Physical Characteristics 31

Characteristics and Qualities 35

Chapter 3 Worldbuilding 44

Where am I? 45

Do Your Research 46

Worldbuilding Chart 49

Describe Primary Residence 49

Map Out Community 49

Surroundings 52

Chapter 4 Murder and Mayhem 55

Setting up the Murder 56

Who is the murderer? 56

How was the victim murdered? 57

Where was the victim murdered? 58

Why was the murder committed? 59

Plotting a Murder...61

Plotting Multiple Murders...70

The Protagonist's Role 71

Accessibility to Crime Scene 72

Example 72

Chapter 5 Creating an Outline...74

Types of Outlines 75

Four-Act Structure 78

Chapter 6 Writing, Editing, Rewriting, Revision and All That Fun Stuff 110

Writing Workday 111

Editing 112

Beta Readers 115

ARC Readers 116

Recap 117

Chapter 7 The Cover... 118

Books Are Judged by Their Cover.................................. 119

What is a vector image?... 120

What are illustrations? 120

Vectors vs Illustrations 121

'Who Killed Mary Christmas' Project 121

Graphic Artists.. 125

Working with Graphic Artists 127

Chapter 8 Pseudonym 132

Choosing an Author Name 133

Chapter 9 Sales Pitch 136

Writing Your Blurb 137

What Is A Blurb? 137

Main Components of a Blurb 145

Chapter 10 Launching Your Book 146

Pre-Order 147

Amazon 147

Goodreads 160

Chapter 11 Advertising 168

Social Proof 169

Amazon – Free Advertising 171

Keywords 171

Categories 181

Amazon – Paid Advertising 193

Setting Up Your Campaign 193

Auto-Targeting 196

Manual Targeting 202

Optimizing Campaigns 212

Facebook or Meta (Snicker) 232

Optimizing Campaigns 246

Thank You for Reading 256

INTRODUCTION

WHY A CHRISTMAS COZY BOOK?

Christmas starts in August. Well, at least for me it does. By August, I'm burning pumpkin spice candles and listening to Christmas music. You see, that's when I begin writing my Christmas mysteries in earnest. The nights are growing cooler, and fall is just around the corner. It's my favorite time of year to figure out how I'm going to murder someone… festively, of course.

SO WHY PICK CHRISTMAS?

There are many reasons. First, Christmas cozies are among the most sought-after mysteries. Readers wait all year for new yuletide mysteries to be released. It's true—mystery readers love Christmas cozies. How do I know? Because I read hundreds of reviews on Amazon, Goodreads and Barnes & Noble, where cozy readers said exactly that.

Aside from their popularity, a lot of worldbuilding is already done for you. Readers want a magical world, alive with vibrant colors, music, friendship, Christmas spirit and murder. A Christmas cozy embodies all these things. It enables you to paint a colorful world filled with greens, reds and golds. You can create a busy little town, sidewalks bustling with shoppers bundled up against the cold, their arms loaded down with shopping bags stuffed with gifts. I bet if you take a second, you can already picture that scene in your mind's eye.

What else do you see? A café? Do you hear the bell jingle as people hurry inside? Can you smell the rich aroma of coffee and fresh-baked pastries swirling through the air? I can too!

From colorful stocking caps to runny red noses, a beautiful world is waiting for you. This is your opportunity to reminisce and revive past Christmases or create the Christmas of your dreams, blending it all into an exciting community—filled with friends, yuletide cheer and murder. You and I together, will work through this wonderful creative writing experience and before you know it, you'll have crafted your first murder mystery.

Whether you are writing for yourself, for your family and friends, or if you want to write to sell, you'll want to put forth your best effort. In the world of cozy mysteries there are certain expectations, even more so with Christmas cozies. Not only are you committing to following the basic tenets of the cozy mystery genre, but you are promising to tell a story filled with Christmas spirit: Hope, Magic, Escapism. Are you ready? Are you excited? Let's do this!

Chapter 1
Christmas Cozy Mystery Writing

RULES AND EXPECTATIONS

Have you ever wanted to murder someone? I know what you're thinking, *That's between me and my therapist. But, while you're on the topic, please, elaborate.* I ask because you are about to embark on a creative journey that allows you to murder in... shall we say, interesting ways—and what better time to murder someone, than Christmas?

"Marty, that eggnog is to *die* for."

"Yes, it is," Marty smiled knowingly. "Have another glass, I see yours is empty."

As a genre, cozy mysteries are deliciously unique and fun to write. I oftentimes find myself giggling aloud in my chair. However, a word of warning, there are certain rules that must be followed. Readers of the cozy genre have certain expectations, and if they aren't met, you will hear about it. You may even get coal in your stockings. You scoff, but it happens.

When writing a Christmas cozy, not only are you committing to the basic tenets of the cozy mystery genre, you are also taking on the added expectation of creating a world filled with Christmas spirit. You've been given the gift of an incredible palette filled with vibrant colors from which to work.

Readers have high expectations. They want to disappear into a world filled with the colors, sights, sounds and smells of Christmas. They want to hear those Christmas tunes, see the lights strung up on houses, smell the coffee and taste the apple cider. They want to become a part of your protagonists' family and community.

It's up to you to deliver. And believe me, they will let you know when you don't, in a very public forum. Part of the research I conducted while writing this book was mulling through hundreds of Christmas murder mystery reviews on Amazon, Goodreads and Barnes & Noble. I wanted to see what readers liked and what they disliked. In the following chapters, I'll dissect the reviews, to make sure you incorporate the must-haves in your mystery.

The following rules are not set in stone. I have read cozy mysteries that *bend* them a little, some more so than others. However, after reading hundreds of reviews, I've found that it is best to follow readers' expectations, and the genre rules as closely as possible.

1 – Family Friendly

Cozy mysteries are generally *family friendly*. There's *no gratuitous violence*, there's *little or no profanity*, and if there is *sex, it's behind closed doors*.

If you want to imply that a couple is engaged in sexual activity, it's sufficient to say: *Chase and Gwynevere disappeared into the bedroom.* There can be hints as to what is about to occur. For example, they can give each other come-hither looks from across the room, (I'm giving you a come-hither look now, do you feel the passion?) or maybe Gwynevere and Chase exit the room—Gwynevere's hair is a mess and Chase's shirt is haphazardly buttoned when they return.

As far as profanity goes, some cozy writers feel comfortable sprinkling in the occasional curse word. I, however, try to keep my books as clean as possible. From a marketing standpoint, this works. A lot of our readers are church-going folk. Since they know our books do not contain sex or profanity, they feel comfortable suggesting our books to others. A large group of cozy readers use keyword phrases such as *clean cozy mysteries* when they search for books on Amazon. There's also another *tiny* reason I don't include these things in my books, my parents read them. They also follow me on social media, I can't catch a break. *Love you Mom and Dad.*

2 – Small Community

Most cozies take place in small rural communities where everyone knows each other. That doesn't mean that it has to be a small fishing village in New England, it simply means the story revolves around a fixed location with a thriving community. Your readers want to get to know the community and the regulars. I'll go into a lot of detail about creating locations and worldbuilding in the next section.

So you can easily picture a thriving community filled with a great supporting cast, I'll give you a couple quick examples. Many people in my generation grew up watching a show called *Cheers*. *Cheers* was about a bar in Boston where a diverse cast of characters met daily to discuss their lives. The entire show was based on their lives and interactions. The show's theme song even included the words "Sometimes you wanna go where everybody knows your name." This show is an exemplary example of a supporting cast that is extremely close and knows quite a bit about one another. The song is a perfect example as well, showing how much audiences want and expect familiarity.

Another creative example of a location that has its own diverse community is *Only Murders in the Building*—a new murder mystery show on Hulu written by Steve Martin and John Hoffman. It takes place in an exclusive Upper West Side apartment building for the wealthy. The story follows three true crime podcasters that only investigate murders that occur in their apartment building. The show follows many of the cozy mystery rules, however, it has quite a bit of profanity.

3 – Murder Is at the Beginning of the Book

The murder *usually* takes place in the first third of the book. This gives the reader plenty of time to investigate along with the amateur sleuth and figure out the crime. It also enables you to add another murder to heighten intrigue and help the pacing of the story should it begin to become bogged down in the middle.

4 – No Gory Murders

Speaking of murder, the readers don't want every gruesome detail (I know I know, I'm a killjoy). A simple explanation will do. That doesn't mean that you can't be creative with the way you kill your victim. Some of the favorite ways for cozy authors to kill their victims are stabbing, poisoning, pushing the victim downstairs, shooting, bludgeoning, drowning and strangulation. Make the murder creative and spectacular but leave out all the gory details.

5 – Multiple Suspects

With too few suspects, you may disappoint your reader if they figure out the mystery too soon. Too many, and the story can get bogged down and confusing. Between four to eight suspects is a good number. Not many of us can handle twelve suspects masterfully like Agatha Christie does in the *Murder on the Orient Express*.

Don't lie to your readers in an effort to hide information. Your readers want a fair shake at solving the mystery along with the protagonist. It's fine to have *red herrings* throughout your story, but don't deliberately give them false information that would preclude them from solving the murder. The reader wants to match wits with you and try to figure out who the killer is. They want to be able to move through the story working one on one with the protagonist. If you hide valuable information, the reader will feel cheated. Sprinkle clues along the way.

WHAT IS A RED HERRING?

Can you give me some examples? Certainly, I'm glad you asked!

A herring is a foraging fish belong to the family Clupeidae. They are usually found in the shallow temperate waters of the North Pacific and North Atlantic Oceans. Wait, what? Oh! Yes of course, you meant the *red herring*. Ahem…, well, that's something different altogether.

The red herring is a literary device that is used to distract the reader from suspecting the real murderer. You can see how this would be a valuable tool in your mystery. It allows you to distract your readers from what's really going on. Let's look at a couple examples.

In Dan Brown's book *The Da Vinci Code*, he masterfully introduces a red herring and even gives us a huge clue, cleverly disguised in Italian. We are led to believe that Bishop Manuel Aringarosa is the head of the Opus Dei sect. Throughout the book, we think he is the mastermind plotting all the evil deeds. However, in the end, we realize it was someone else. Why was this such a clever red herring? The bishop's name, *Aringarosa* when translated from Italian means "*aringa*" herring and "*rosa*" red. Put them together and we get red herring.

In the book *The Prisoner of Azkaban* by J.K. Rowling, we are led to believe that Sirius Black is the man who murdered Harry Potter's family. Harry believes that Sirius Black is looking for him to kill him. We later find out that this isn't true, that Sirius Black loves him and is there to protect him. Red herrings enable you to lead the reader astray and then surprise them when the truth is revealed.

6 – Convincing Reason for the Amateur to Investigate

Create a compelling reason for your amateur sleuth to get involved. Were they planting a new garden and discover a body in their backyard? Did Santa collapse after taking a drink of eggnog? Was he murdered or did he forget to check the expiration date?

7 – Murders Made Simple

Cozies can have complex plots, but they usually don't get involved in topics such as human trafficking, international terrorist groups or crime syndicates. They focus on community, friendship, good storytelling, and murders. Don't forget the murders.

8 – A Fulfilling Conclusion

Your cozy mystery should be a complete story with a murder, a trail of clues, and a satisfying ending whereupon the murderer is caught, justice is served up like a freshly baked loaf of bread, and the community returns to a state of normalcy.

These are the basic guidelines. Make sure you follow them as you write your mystery, and your readers will thank you.

WHAT READERS *WANT* FROM A CHRISTMAS MYSTERY

Before you begin crafting your mystery, I think that it's a good idea to understand your audience. A great way to do this is to go to your local bookstore and skulk around the murder mystery section and… okay, I apologize, don't do that. A great way to figure out what your readers want in your specific genre is to *read through the reviews of authors in your genre*. Reviewers will give you a tremendous insight into their likes and dislikes.

As I mentioned earlier, as I was researching for this book, I combed through hundreds of reviews of cozy Christmas murders. Here, in their own words, is what your audience wants. Let's look at some of them together.

- ***I loved all the characters** and the **Christmas magic**!*
- *This has everything Christmassy and more! **I love, love, love the setting** and the names of the **people** and **places**.*
- ***Sweet**, **funny story** in a **wonderful winter and holiday setting**.*
- *A **delightful fun** cozy read. I'll be **waiting for the next**.*
- *If you want to get in the **Christmas mode** read this book!!! I really enjoyed reading this book!!! **Merry Christmas to you all**!*
- ***I want to move to Candy Cane Hollow**. It sounds **magical**, just what we need this year. The **characters** and **settings** are great.*
- *Truly **Christmas magic**!!*
- *I gave this book a **high rating** because **it held my interest** with **fun characters** and a **good clean mystery to figure out**.*

- *I did **have my Christmas lights on, most of the time**, and **I enjoyed a cup of peppermint cocoa turning a bad night into a festive reading escape**. I totally **recommend** this book!*
- *A murder in a **beautiful winter wonderland**. I absolutely **adore this cozy Christmas mystery**. I **highly recommend** Christmas Corpse as a great read any time, but especially during the **holiday season**. Who knows? You might just **rediscover the magic of Christmas**!*
- *What a **magical** start to a wonderful new series.*
- ***Cozy Christmas Perfection. Can't wait for the next book**!*
- ***Delicious recipes** are also included in the book.*
- *I **loved** this **magical town** and **everyone** in it.*
- *I was even **feeling** more **Christmassy** after reading it. **I can't wait for the next book**!*
- *I **adore Christmas-themed books**. I **eagerly wait for them all year**, especially the books that are a **part of a series**.*
- ***Interesting characters** and **twists** to **keep me guessing** added to the **fun***.
- *If you haven't yet, you'll want to **catch up with the first two books in the series** as well. They all do well as standalone, but **you'll want the whole story, I promise**!*
- *A **merry mix** of **mistletoe** and murder!*
- *I could **feel myself wandering through the snow, baking tons of amazing treats**, and **thinking about ways to gift wrap with elegance**. Frost **truly immerses you in the setting**, and this makes for a **special reading treat**. I like the **progression with the characters** and the overall **story was filled with a bunch of red herrings** and **interesting clues**.*
- *I **love the setting, characters** and the **recipes sound delicious**. I can't wait to try them.*

- *It was the overall **feeling of the holiday** that made me **love** this book.*

I've bolded the words that express how readers feel about the Christmas mysteries they've read. I've addressed each of the keywords from their reviews, and written explanations as to why they're important.

Christmas Magic

The feeling of Christmas is definitely unique. There is no other time during the year quite like it. Readers want a book filled with all things *Christmassy*. I would encourage you to use your five senses when creating a world that is *Christmassy*. Incorporate the vivid colors, Christmas carols, the smell of firewood burning, the feeling of a scratchy wool sweater, the taste of freshly baked Christmas cookies.

EXERCISE

It's Christmas Eve and you've just stepped into a busy café. Using your five senses, describe the environment. How are people dressed? What's the atmosphere like? Are people congregating in groups talking? Is there music? Is there a roaring fire? You can download the exercises from this book at christmascozymystery.com/resources.

_____

_____

_____

_____

_____

_____

_____

_____

_____

_____

Setting and People

Readers described the settings as magical over and over. The reviewers loved the characters. Create a community that the reader can envision. Create meaningful interactions among the characters. Don't create paper-thin characters that are as boring to write as they are to read. Small communities are often filled with colorful, quirky people.

Sweet – Funny – Clean

Again, create fun characters. Keep an eye on the use of profanity.

EXAMPLE OF A FUN CHARACTER

Let's create a person named Simon. How can we make him exciting? Maybe Simon's granddaughter bought him a new high-tech hearing aid. It's new to the market and was supposedly developed by a retired CIA covert operative. She told him that it's supposed to be the best of the best and that it uses new technology.

At first, Simon thought he was going crazy because he kept hearing voices in his head. But then, he realizes at the local café that his new-fangled hearing aid can hear people's cellphone conversations.

Now this feisty octogenarian is getting all the juicy gossip. He begins writing a gossip column under the fictitious name of Wilma Brite for the local paper, revealing all the scandalous details of the calls he hears. He's murdered when someone figures out who he is, for overhearing something he shouldn't.

There you go, that's a quick and fun cozy to write. The entire town could be suspects.

I Can't Wait for the Next Book

Perfect! Thrilled reviewers are eager for your next book. This is the best social proof you can get. When readers recommend your books to others, it validates your book.

Able to Disappear Into the Book

This is another amazing compliment. When you are able to write a book that enables readers to disappear from reality and become a part of your imaginary world, then you've done your job as a writer.

Changing People's Lives

The ability to change people's lives is also another amazing feat. This reader says: I was even *feeling* more *Christmassy* after reading it. *I enjoyed a cup of peppermint cocoa turning a bad night into a festive reading escape.* These readers recommended the book because it allowed them to escape, and to feel better. Add a *delicious recipe* into the mix and not only are people reading your book, but also interacting with it!

In reality, books can bring about physiological changes in our readers. I know that I want to bring laughter, joy and happiness into my readers' lives, don't you?

WHAT READERS *DON'T* WANT FROM A CHRISTMAS MYSTERY

Now, let's take a look at some of the things readers *don't* want. Here are some of their reviews.

- *The reason for the 4 stars versus 5 had to do with the **need for a bit of editing**. Heavens knows that I realize how hard it is to get that sort of thing perfect, but **it did occasionally make me have to reread a sentence or two**.*
- *The **main character**, [Removed to protect the author] preparing for an over-the-top Christmas, **comes off as a nitwit**. **I didn't care about any of the characters**. They were **cartoonish**. And the **murder doesn't happen until page 114**, which is **more than a 3rd of the way into the silly book**. I usually love Christmas backdrops, but this doesn't work at all. **Not recommended**.*
- *I used to really enjoy the books in this series, however, the last few have **really gone downhill**. It's as though **someone different is writing them**, perhaps a child. The **dialogue is very clipped**, and the **details are very mundane**. **We spend pages and pages reading about every little ingredient for every little thing they are going to put in their mouth**. There are more chapters talking about the ingredients of their food than there are about the plot of the mystery. This could have been a 30-page short story.*

***60 people found this helpful**

I included the amount of people that found the last review helpful because I want to discuss how this impacts the sale of your book.

Amazon uses the *helpful* trigger as a way to determine the popularity of a review.

It's another important marker you need to be aware of. When a lot of people mark a bad review as *helpful*, Amazon gives more weight to the review because of engagement. Since so many people marked this review as being helpful, Amazon will give it a more prominent position on the page.

So, if you have a one-star review, and a lot of people found it helpful, it will move to a more eye-catching spot at the top of your reviews. This is why it is incredibly important to *know your genre* and provide them with an *exceptionally written book*.

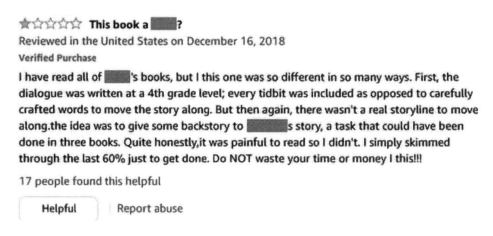

★☆☆☆☆ **This book a** ▮▮▮▮**?**
Reviewed in the United States on December 16, 2018
Verified Purchase

I have read all of ▮▮▮▮'s books, but I this one was so different in so many ways. First, the dialogue was written at a 4th grade level; every tidbit was included as opposed to carefully crafted words to move the story along. But then again, there wasn't a real storyline to move along.the idea was to give some backstory to ▮▮▮▮▮s story, a task that could have been done in three books. Quite honestly,it was painful to read so I didn't. I simply skimmed through the last 60% just to get done. Do NOT waste your time or money I this!!!

17 people found this helpful

Helpful   Report abuse

How do I do that? By doing your due diligence. When I first began writing, my first few books were filled with grammatical errors. I hired a big-name professional editor, and I did everything he suggested. After several edits he said my book was ready to be published. I took him at his word and uploaded my manuscript to Amazon. It didn't take long for the one-star reviews to come rolling in. Within a week, I had dozens of reviewers complaining about misspellings, repetitive word usage, character name changes… it was bad. I couldn't understand why my editor would have said, 'Ready to publish.' Maybe he meant, 'Ready to publish?'

I hired another editor, and she tore my book apart. Literally, she mailed me back the book in pieces. Okay, of course I'm kidding, but in reality, she found over 400 errors. Thankfully, she wrote a forty-page summation of all the things that were incorrectly done—I believe it was longer than my book. Her outline made me angry—she took my ego, my pride, rolled it up into a little ball and drop kicked it through the field goal of failure. She won the game 7 to 0.

After about a week of wallowing in self-pity, I began to realize how valuable her advice was. I reworked the manuscript, and I hired a group of beta readers to analyze the story and give me feedback. Again, this was a lesson in humiliation, but I realized that all this work was making my story better. After reworking and republishing my book, those one and two stars went away and were replaced by four- and five-star reviews. Toward the end of this book, I talk about my editing and review process. I hope that you will read that section carefully and give it a lot of thought. Working with beta readers and ARC (Advanced Reader Copy) readers is one of the most pleasurable parts of the editing process.

Let's take a look at some Christmas cozies that received bad reviews. I've bolded key points for us to discuss in each example.

- *Ridiculous story, oops, I meant to say **ridiculous lack of plot**. **Shallow, one-dimensional characters**.*
- *This is a **boring cozy mystery**. **Protagonist repeats herself over-and-over**. My late father was a letter carrier (in Manhattan, not Montana), and I found **too many mistakes in the heroine's job***

actions. *I also found the protagonist **dull-witted**. I liked the supporting character, but **disliked her so-called best friend, supporting character**. **Convoluted clues** and eventual **blah answer to the killing didn't go anywhere**. **Not recommended**.*

- *The main story is engaging. **The book could use a good editor**. There are some oddities throughout the book with **words that don't fit like the author doesn't know what they mean**. At another point the word "digest" was **replaced by "disgust"** as in "how we were going to try to help her **disgust this huge blow**. Finally, if you write a series, **keep track of the details you give**.*

- *I liked the book, **but it needs some editing**. There were **missing words** in a few places that were **quite distracting**. Otherwise it was a good book. **Had it been properly edited I would have added a star**.*

- *I like the stories, plot line moves along at a good pace, **but there are a lot of typos**. **Not misspelled words**, rather **extra words, missing words and bad grammar**.*

- *The **characters are fun and interesting**. I really wish more time would be taken with the editing. The **typos** and **errors** in the storyline **are very distracting**.*

- *I am enjoying these stories, the characters are fun, and the plots are engaging, but the **editing gets worse with each one**. They're **basic** and **obvious mistakes**. I'm **not sure why they haven't been corrected**. **It's frustrating**, but I'm reading them anyways because **they're clean and easy reads** and that's not always easy to find!*

- *The story itself was cute and I like the characters. However, the book had **many errors including missing words, incorrect words, and the sentence structure was difficult to understand sometimes**.*

- *This was my first read by this author. I enjoyed the story and characters. **The only complaint…too many spelling errors**.*

Let's break down the main complaints, so we can steer away from them as we create our Christmas mystery together.

Character Development

Developing well-rounded, interesting characters is one of the most important elements of your story. Remember, cozies are based around a small community and a small cast of characters. If they are annoying or cartoonish, people will not be able to relate, and they won't want to spend time with them. Work on creating well-developed, appealing characters. Remember the details from the reviews and the way they described the characters: Cartoonish, shallow, one-dimensional.

Think about your community and cast of supporting characters this way. If you wouldn't want to spend time with them, neither will your readers.

Amateur Sleuth as the Protagonist

People want a protagonist that they can relate to. Remember, your reader will be shoulder to shoulder with your protagonist—hopefully, rooting them along as they work to solve the murder. Yes, your protagonist should be quirky, and broken and evolving, but don't make them a stumbling buffoon.

Make sure you do your research when it comes to your protagonist's vocation or hobbies. If your protagonist is a mailman, do the leg work. Go to your local post office and interview actual postal workers. Learn everything you can on the internet. If your protagonist is a florist, then you need to learn everything involved with running a floral shop (And

I'll expect chocolates on Valentine's and a lovely bouquet of flowers on my birthday. Daisies are my favorite).

Murder Happened Too Late or Was Disappointing

First, I would like to say, I hate it when murders are disappointing. Cozy readers like to have the murder occur in the first act, or the first quarter of the book. This allows them to begin solving the murder right away. It also allows your reader to see how the amateur sleuth is going to become involved and why. At this point, your reader will be asking a lot of questions. Who killed the victim? How will the protagonist become involved? Why are they involved? Why are they motivated to solve the case? How will they get access to clues, to witnesses? This is where the story becomes exciting for the reader, don't make them wait too long!

Editing Blunders

Nothing annoys readers more than being pulled out of a story over and over by bad editing. Poor editing can destroy your book, lead to horrible reviews and less stars on Amazon and Goodreads. Not only are you annoying your readers, but you are leaving them frustrated. Another common theme is being distracted. You don't want your reader to feel distracted because they are continually pulled from the story.

In a nutshell, here are the main complaints from readers so far:

"Book needs a better editor." "A lot of typos…" "Very distracting." "Editing gets worse each time." "Author used the wrong words or misused words." "Missing words, incorrect words, grammar and sentence structure problems." "Too many spelling errors."

I may ruffle a few feathers here, but I don't recommend self-editing. Sure, there are a few writers that can do this well, but I've seen far too many self-edited books that are atrocious. Your readers deserve quality. They demand it. I want to plant the seed that you'll want to think about an editor and beta readers. I'll discuss this in greater detail in later chapters. There's a great meme going around the internet, and it shows why people may want to reconsider self-editing.

What I If told you
You the read first line wrong
Same the with second
And also the third

Overly Complex Plot Line

"The book was confusing" → This usually happens with a convoluted plot line or poor planning. I'll cover this more when I discuss developing your outline and plot.

"Author didn't keep track of details" → Again, this can be fixed if you create a detailed outline.

"Convoluted clues" → Create clues that enable your reader to take note and follow along with your amateur sleuth. Remember cozy readers love the thrill of figuring out the mystery before the protagonist. Make sure you give them a pathway to achieve this, but not too early of course.

Dissatisfying Ending

"Hi James. What book are you reading?"

"Great Expectations."

"How is it?" asked Mary.

"It's not all I was hoping for," James replied.

"I just finished a book, and the **ending was a complete let down**. There was a lot of **feverish action and confusion**, and after **re-reading the ending three times**, I still can't visualize how they trapped the murderer. It was definitely a *meh* moment for me."

Cozy readers want a clever reveal, but they also need some danger and drama involved. They'll also need to be able to visualize it. Some points you'll want to think about as you craft your story:

❧ How will your protagonist confront the murderer?

❧ If their life is in danger, how do they escape?

❧ How is the murderer captured?

Make the reveal and the capture exciting. And once that's done, make sure the miscreant is properly punished! Justice must be served, and our protagonist is able to return to some semblance of a normal life. Peace and prosperity are returned to the community, and our readers anxiously await another trip to your town.

Poor Dialogue

I've read too many books where the author thinks they are the funniest thing on two legs. Don't overthink funny. Don't try to force funny. Everyday life is funny if you watch for it. There are little blips of odd human behavior everywhere we look.

EXAMPLE This morning I pulled into the parking lot between two cars to drop my daughter off for school. I noticed that the two cars on either side of me had their windows down, and the two women had been deep in conversation (Which I interrupted). I waved to them and backed up several feet so they could continue talking. They both thought that simple gesture was hilarious, and they went back to shouting to each other.

Dialogue Doesn't Flow

Be interesting and move the story forward. Read your dialogue aloud. Does it flow? Does it go on forever without getting anywhere? Does it perhaps reveal some information or clues that are necessary to moving the story forward? Dialogue can be an extremely useful tool, fill it with action to propel your story forward.

THE DEATH KNELL

"I don't recommend this book" → You definitely don't want that comment appearing in your reviews. Follow the cozy guidelines and the advice offered in this book, and you will be well on your way to avoiding negative reviews.

That being said, your writing style will *never* make everyone happy, no matter how hard you try. What you can do however is make sure you give them very little to be unhappy about. Write the best story you can. Pour your heart and soul into it, and then edit, edit and edit again! Your readers will thank you, and you'll be proud of your work! Onward and upward!

Chapter 2
Amateur Sleuth

A FEW EXAMPLES OF FAMOUS SLEUTHS

Hercule Poirot

Imagine creating a character that is so beloved, the New York Times featured his obituary on the front page. Famed Belgian detective Hercule Poirot is the man, and Agatha Christie, his creator.

Human beings by nature are curious. We love mysteries, the unknown. We also like to align ourselves with people that make us feel good about ourselves. No one knew this better than Agatha Christie. Two of her most beloved protagonists Jane Marple and Hercule Poirot appeared in nearly fifty novels and over sixty short stories. Aside from the Bible and Shakespeare, no one has come close to selling as many books as Agatha Christie with over two billion sold around the world.

Agatha Christie's characters had depth. They grew, they learned, they aged, and they prospered. Hercule Poirot's wealth continued to grow with each case that he solved. Agatha created a backstory for her characters. Poirot was a Belgian refugee from World War I and began his career as a police officer. Agatha used his knowledge of police and investigation procedures to help him later when he becomes a private investigator. She also made him highly intelligent and a bit of an egomaniac. Poirot often solved his cases with a dramatic dénouement in front of a crowd of people. As he solved more and more crimes, he became increasingly wealthy, which increased his exposure to the world and enabled him to travel and solve crimes in more exotic places.

Christie also humanized him and gave him some quirky flaws, enabling us to see his imperfections. Much of this was done in a comedic way. For example, in the *Murder on the Orient Express*, she described Poirot as "a little man with enormous mustaches." She also described him as having an egg-shaped head.

Speaking of characters, Poirot's mustache began to gain ground as a supporting character moving from gigantic to immense and then amazing. Agatha even introduced a tiny pair of curling tongs to give his mustache that upward swoop at the end, perfectly fitting for such a glorious mustache. Bravo!

Jane Marple

Miss Marple's character was a mixture of Agatha's step-grandmother and her grandmother's friends. Miss Marple's character evolved from a town gossip to an intelligent conversationalist that was an astute observer of human behavior. If we delve into her background, we find out that she had a thorough education, including art courses that involved the study of human anatomy using human cadavers. In the book *They Do it With Mirrors*, we learn that she studied in an Italian finishing school.

Miss Marple was such a popular character that she was the protagonist in twelve Agatha Christie novels, numerous short stories and appeared on television and the big screen.

Sherlock Holmes

Author Conan Doyle wrote four novels and fifty-six short stories about Sherlock Holmes. Here we find an ingenious man who is an intolerable pompous jerk. Sherlock even refers to himself as a high-functioning sociopath. In the world of Sherlock Holmes, it's his stunning intellect and his flaws that make him utterly fascinating. Readers are even willing to brush his use of narcotics in *A Study in Scarlet*. The number of spinoffs from Sherlock's character is mind-boggling. From plays, to books, to graphic novels to movies, this beloved character is one of the most influential detectives ever.

Alvirah and Willy

Mary Higgins Clark, whom I absolutely love, wrote over 80 novels. Eleven books had two reoccurring protagonists, Alvirah and Willy, a lottery winner and her husband, who used their winnings to solve crimes. Her books are exceptionally well-written and plotted, and her characters are exceptionally well-developed. If you get a chance, pick up a copy.

Interestingly, several of the books with Alvirah and Willy are Christmas-themed books: *All Through the Night*, *Deck the Halls*, *The Christmas Thief*, and *Dashing Through the Snow*. I'm currently reading and enjoying *The Christmas Thief*.

CREATING YOUR AMATEUR SLEUTH

Before we begin the amateur sleuth creation process, let's make sure we nail down the key components of amateur sleuthdom.

The Protagonist Should Be Relatable

It's important to remember your main protagonist is an *amateur sleuth*. This is not a book about the intricacies of police procedure or forensics. This is a book about a normal citizen who is compelled or forced to step in and solve a murder.

A lot of new authors have problems moving past this. They want to make sure they get the homicide, crime scene and all the intricate details of the investigation down. You need to understand that cozy readers are able to suspend their beliefs as part of the genre. Think about James Bond, or Ethan Hunt in *Mission Impossible*. We are constantly asked to suspend our beliefs in the laws of physics as the hero performs impossible rescues. My favorite is watching a hero hang by one hand off the runner of a helicopter, while holding onto another person with their other hand. Most people can't even support their own weight with both hands.

Don't worry, cozy readers don't expect your character to be well versed in the law of the land and the intricacies of forensics and police investigations.

Your Protagonist Should Have Some Flaws

They should be *human* and have a few quirks to add depth and richness to your character, but don't go overboard. These quirks and flaws humanize your protagonist and help your reader to connect with them. Here are a few flaws your sleuth may have:

Forgetful	Claustrophobic	Moody
Casanova	Self-sabotaging	Abrasive
Dramatic	Whiny (Not excessive)	Obsessive
Haughty	Perfectionist	Paranoid
Narcissistic	Introverted	Manipulative

Healthy Supporting Cast

Your sleuth needs to have enough interaction with the community to have a routine where they come into contact with a lot of people. The more social interaction, the more opportunities you have to create numerous situations for murders and multiple suspects. Remember, your amateur sleuth will need to have a plethora of people to investigate and question. Investigative questioning is one of the key ways your protagonist and reader will get the information they need to solve the murder.

So, where do I start? Grab a pen and then visit the following website: christmascozymystery.com/resources. There, you will find amateur sleuth creation charts with more descriptors than are listed here. Print a few off, and then we'll continue. If you don't have access to a printer right now, it's okay. I've given you space in the book where you can write your answers.

Do you have a main protagonist in mind? If you close your eyes for a moment, can you see them? Maybe your amateur sleuth reminds you of someone in your family. Perhaps they remind you of a friend, or an actor, maybe a combination of multiple people. There is no wrong answer.

Let's begin filling out the chart together (Even if you don't have a character in mind yet, this is a great exercise).

BASICS

Name	
Gender	
Birthdate	
Age	
Birthplace	
Ethnicity	
Height	
Weight	

PHYSICAL CHARACTERISTICS

Start with their hair and work your way down to their feet. Don't worry, I'm about to go through an incredible amount of detail. You may only have a few characteristics at this point, that's perfectly fine. Over time, you will fill in your sleuth creation chart with more details. Right now, I simply want you to have a basic guideline established as you develop your character.

Hair

Do they have long hair? Short hair? Wavy hair? What color is it? Is it dyed or color-treated? Is it thick? Lustrous? Thinning? Are they bald? Do they wear a toupee? Do they wear a hat to hide their baldness? Do they like wearing hats? What type?

_____

_____

_____

Eyebrows

Are they thin or big and bushy? Are they penciled in, or turning gray with age? Does your protagonist dye them? Do they get Botox and their eyebrows are permanently arched upward making them always look surprised? (I'm asking for a friend.)

_____

_____

_____

_____

Eyes

What color are they? What shape? Are they close together or set far apart? Does your protagonist wear contact lenses or glasses? Do they blink a lot? What's their vision like? Would it be traumatic for them if they were to lose their glasses? Do they wear reading glasses?

_____

_____

_____

_____

Ears

Small? Large? Pierced? Hearing aid?

_____

_____

_____

Nose

What shape is their nose? Is it long and narrow? Short and stubby? Is it crooked? Do they have a nose piercing? Does their nose whistle?

_____

_____

_____

_____

Lips

Are they full? Thin and narrow? Pale, pink, rosy-red? Do they wear lipstick? Does your protagonist have a habit of licking them, or chewing on their bottom lip?

_____

_____

_____

_____

Face Overall

Wrinkled forehead? Age spots? Rosy cheeks? Smile lines? Crow's feet? Piercings? Birthmarks? High cheekbone? Pointy chin? Dimples? Freckles? Adult acne?

_____

_____

_____

_____

Facial Hair

No facial hair? Five o'clock shadow? Beard? Mustache? Goatee? Color of facial hair? Sideburns? Soul Patch? (Also known as the jazz dab or jazz dot or mouche. Thank you, Google.)

_____

_____

_____

_____

Body Type

Pear-shaped? Thin? A few extra pounds? Overweight? Petite? Massive upper body with tiny little legs?

_____

_____

_____

_____

Physical

Athletic? Couch potato? Weekend warrior? Walk with a limp? Stiff shoulders? Arthritis? Walks with a cane? Thin and wiry? Muscular?

_____

_____

_____

_____

Tattoos and Piercings

If they have tattoos, what and where are they? Do they have a story behind them? Piercings? What and where?

_____

_____

_____

_____

Jewelry

Do they have a sentimental watch? A necklace or locket that has been passed down for generations? Or perhaps your protagonist wears their mother or grandmother's wedding ring.

_____

_____

_____

_____

CHARACTERISTICS AND QUALITIES

Now that you have a basic physical description, let's take a look at what's going on between their ears.

Personality

Are they a social butterfly, able to ease into any conversation? Are they hotheaded and they're taking anger management classes? Are they introspective, an introvert? Do they suffer from social anxiety and don't do well in crowds? Are they easygoing? A know-it-all? Do they have phobias? Are they afraid of water? Are they claustrophobic? Afraid of spiders? Do they have superstitions? Are they a neat freak and can't stand any type of clutter?

_____

_____

_____

_____

_____

_____

Do They Have Quirks or Interesting Mannerisms?

As I travel, I like to people-watch and pick up on eccentric behavior. For example, in the book *A Garden to Die For*, I talk about a woman who sits in a restaurant and goes through a ritual of straightening her silverware, aligning them just so, then folding her napkin just so and placing it on her lap. People can be quirky. Another example is a jogger in our neighborhood, with every other stride, he brings his right fist up to his nose and sniffs it.

_____

_____

_____

_____

_____

_____

_____

How Do They Speak?

Softly? Slowly? Rapid fire? Do they have rich tones? Deep voice? High-pitched? Do they have a southern twang, or are they from New England with a bit more of an edge? Do they stutter? Are they from a different country from where you currently reside?

_____

_____

_____

_____

_____

Hobbies and Interests

Do they like to shoot pool or hoops? Do they run a couple miles after work or run to the local bar or café with their friends? Do they play the piano or paint? Do they meditate or garden? Perhaps they're in a reading club or they love to bake. It can really be anything: stamp collecting, knitting, composing, birdwatching, kayaking, the opportunities are endless. One or two small pastimes are needed to develop your protagonist. These should be considered separate to their abilities and experience that make them a good sleuth.

_____

_____

_____

_____

_____

What Is Their Relationship Status?

Are they single? Recently divorced or widowed? Looking to meet someone? Engaged? Girlfriend or boyfriend?

_____

_____

_____

_____

_____

_____

_____

How Is Your Character Broken?

No one's life is perfect. Have they recently lost a loved one? Has their pet of 15 years just died? Has their last child left for college and suddenly the house is empty and quiet? Did they go through a divorce? Were they recently fired? Do they feel unfulfilled? Do they have a parent who has a disability or under their care? What makes them human?

_____

_____

_____

_____

_____

_____

How Are They Trying to Grow?

Do they read a lot? Are they engaging with new people? Taking an online course or a class at the local college? Are they a podcast aficionado—perhaps a crime story podcast nerd? Are they learning a foreign language or taking cooking classes?

_____

_____

_____

_____

_____

_____

_____

_____

Likes and Dislikes

This can be anything from food to music. Have fun with this.

WARNING Stay away from the political arena; you will always offend at least half of your readers. You will also need to be careful when discussing religion. It is okay to have your protagonist go to church or pray, but if you become too preachy, it can become offensive.

When is it okay to discuss religion in more detail? If you are writing a religious cozy murder mystery or perhaps your amateur sleuth is a minister or priest. Tom Bosley (most people remember him as Howard Cunningham from *Happy Days*) played a priest/detective in the *Father*

Dowling Mysteries. There are several religious cozy mystery series that do quite well.

_____

_____

_____

_____

_____

_____

_____

What Is Their Job?

Do they still have a job? Are they interviewing for one? Are they retired? Are they retired but working part-time just to have something to do? Research their job and make sure you know what it entails. Try to create a job that will bring the protagonist into contact with a lot of people.

_____

_____

_____

_____

_____

_____

_____

Do They Have a Routine?

Do they wake up, shower, and go to the local bakery or café to get a breakfast sandwich and coffee? Do they get up and walk Charlie their dog? Do they do Tai Chi or yoga on the beach?

_____

_____

_____

_____

_____

_____

_____

In *A Mummy to Die For*, we meet forty-year-old Michael West who's trying to adapt to his new life in the small coastal town of Lana Cove, North Carolina. For many years, Michael had been obsessed with work at a distinguished marketing firm in Boston. He believed the long hours and late nights were simply the sacrifices that had to be made to provide for his family. In the end, he lost his wife and before he knew it, his daughter had left for college.

In an attempt to start anew, Michael sells his expensive Boston townhouse and car and uses the money to buy a beautiful house in Lana Cove. He has always wanted to be a writer, and now, the opportunity feels right. Michael finds that without all the pressure and stress, a new person begins to emerge. He finds himself taking long drives by the ocean, enjoying people-watching on the boardwalk, and leisurely enjoying a cup of well-made coffee. He meets Ellie, co-owner of the Bittersweet Café. She befriends him and introduces him to her quirky yet loyal group of friends.

Each day, Michael feels his old self melting away. The salty air and warm sun awaken his soul, rejuvenating him. With a renewed vigor, he begins focusing on his passion, writing. Day by day, he's learning how to live again, and with Ellie in his life, maybe love again.

SPOILER ALERT So how does he get involved in a murder?

With every good story there must be conflict. In the book, *A Mummy to Die For*, Michael feels minimized by an over-the-top gorgeous archeologist, Hugo, who has just discovered a famous mummy and is holding a pre-launch exhibit in Lana Cove.

Ellie becomes swept up in all the fanfare surrounding the exhibit. He becomes insanely jealous when Hugo asks her to be his date for the grand opening. We feel for him as Hugo parades Ellie around on his arm and belittles Michael at every opportunity. Michael becomes involved when Hugo is murdered, and Ellie becomes a suspect.

Again, I know that is a lot of detail! I certainly don't expect you to have all the answers, but I do hope the questions and the suggestions have your mind spinning. Your protagonist chart *will* help you. Plus, if you decide to write a series, you won't have to keep going through your manuscript to remember if Michael had a tattoo of his daughter's name on his right arm or left arm.

PROTAGONIST GROWTH POTENTIAL

Your protagonist charts will become very important to you. As you write, your main character will continue to grow and evolve. The protagonist charts are a great way to see where they are, and where they're going.

You'll be able to use this chart for every character. Don't worry, you don't have to use the chart for minor characters. Minor characters who appear only in passing will only need a few descriptors.

So far, you've created a physical and psychological profile of your protagonist. As you write your story, you'll fill in more details about your main character. Once you've established your main characters, you can begin worldbuilding, which just happens to be the next chapter!

Chapter 3
Worldbuilding

WHERE AM I?

Most people don't like to be lost. They like familiarity and convenience. It's why we use the same brands over and over, shop at the same stores and drive the same way to work every day. We like routines—it makes us feel safe.

Cozy readers like the same thing. They want to be able to envision their protagonist in a familiar environment, doing familiar things surrounded by familiar faces. (I get paid $5 every time I use the word *familiar* by the Familiarity Committee of New England. Thank you, Noah and Margarette, keep those checks coming!)

Your cozy community is the place where your readers will visit over and over. So, you'll want to create an environment that you enjoy writing about because it will be the reoccurring foundation behind each of your stories.

Picture your community in your mind. Do you want to create a New England coastal community with its rocky beaches, cool fall nights, colorful trees and snowy winters? Or perhaps you like the sun, and you want your book to take place in a retirement village in Florida. Both are fine!

Let your imagination run free. You could run a popular bed and breakfast or be a tenant in a high-end apartment building in New York. Your mystery could take place at a ski resort in Vail, or an island resort. Get creative! Just make sure you create a tight, interconnected community with colorful supporting characters that interact with your protagonist.

DO YOUR RESEARCH

When you first begin developing your community, you can simply jot down some simple ideas. For example, Lana Cove is a fictional small coastal town located on the border of Virginia and North Carolina. Where will my protagonist live in this town? Where will they work? What type of daily routine do they have?

Just by asking these three questions you can begin to build out your community.

1 – Where Does My Protagonist Live?

In a house? Condo? Apartment? You can begin to build out a very simple neighborhood. Do they have neighbors? Do they have a fence? Do they live in a neighborhood?

2 – Where Do They Work?

From home? Café? Hotel? Floral Shop? Hair Salon? If they work from home, I advise you to give your protagonist a local hangout or two where they are interacting with locals.

3 – What Is Their Daily Routine?

Do they walk their dog with their neighbors? In my neighborhood, the parents all meet up at the bus stop. Once the children board the bus, they all go for a walk together. Perhaps your protagonist meets up with his best friend at a coffee shop or a restaurant for breakfast every morning. Think about their routine, this will help you add a lot of details to your community.

IMPORTANT Once you have an idea as to the community you are going to create, then make sure you do your research.

If you decide to write about a retirement villa, then learn what you can about retirement community life. If it's about a bed and breakfast, then Google search '*how to run a bed and breakfast*' or '*how to start a bed and breakfast.*' I just did a quick search and there are dozens of informative resources on the topic of opening a bed and breakfast.

If I were basing my book on a bed and breakfast, I would visit a couple, spend the night and interview the owners. Doing detailed research will pay off big in the long run.

I'm often asked if the location has to be an actual location. The answer is no. In *The Coffee House Sleuths* books, the protagonist lives in a small coastal community in North Carolina named Lana Cove. This is a make-believe community. However, that doesn't mean that I can't sprinkle in places that actually exist nearby, like Virginia Beach or Wilmington, North Carolina, or other small towns.

If you decide to use a real location, be sure to include some local landmarks. You'll instantly create a local fanbase who will be excited to read about street names and landmarks they are all familiar with. Also, if you are using a real location, check to see if they have any Christmas festivities such as a parade or festival.

A great way to market your book and involve your readers is to create a travel journal. As you research towns and venues for your book, take pictures of your journey. Eat at a local restaurant, snap pictures of the menu and your meal. If you get a chance, snap a picture with the staff or the owner. It will add more validity to your book. Locals will enjoy seeing their community and readers will appreciate the fact that you researched for your book.

As you write more books in your series, start a board on Pinterest.com, highlighting your research and places that you visited in a series of pictures. If you build a nice following on Pinterest, they'll be anxious to read your next book. Ask your captive audience on Pinterest for restaurants, museums or local attractions that you should visit while you're there. Many times, local hotels, bed and breakfast locations and private businesses will help promote your book.

Does my protagonist have to always stay in the community? No, just like in real life, your protagonist may have to travel for work, or perhaps go on vacation. I wouldn't do this too often because your readers want to read more about the community you've created and engage with the characters. But every once in a while, it's okay to have your protagonist solve a murder on a train, cruise ship or even an island or snowy getaway!

Once you establish a location, you'll need to create the town. I've created a helpful chart with the ordinary things you'd find in a town. For now, you'll be able to fill in the basics, and as you expand your series, you can add more shops and such.

WORLDBUILDING CHART

DESCRIBE PRIMARY RESIDENCE

Here are some of the descriptors you will need to flesh out to describe the residence of your protagonist. I've included an example so you can create the house for your amateur sleuth. You can download the example at christmascozymystery.com/resources.

- ❀ Is the protagonist's house one story or two stories?
- ❀ Is it brick?
- ❀ Does it have a cupola?
- ❀ Does it have a deck on the back or a Florida room?
- ❀ Is it a townhouse or an apartment?
- ❀ Many stories make heavy use of the kitchen. It's the perfect place for neighbors or friends to gather and discuss the murder over a cup of tea or coffee. Describe this area.
- ❀ Does the house have a garage?
- ❀ Is it a lakefront house?
- ❀ Is it in a neighborhood surrounded by other houses?
- ❀ How is it furnished?
- ❀ Is it hardwood flooring or carpeted?

MAP OUT COMMUNITY

You'll want to create a vibrant community. Remember, communities have routines, just like our everyday jobs. Trash pickup on Wednesday. Mail delivery every day except Sunday. On an average day, there are delivery trucks, police vehicles, school buses, ambulances, firetrucks, foot traffic, bicyclists, people driving to work, there is a constant ebb and flow of activity.

Plot out a map of the community. In my books, *The Coffee House Sleuths*, the protagonist lives in a rancher with a cupola that has an ocean view. He uses the cupola as his office.

Michael's house is in Lana Cove, North Carolina, and is about a quarter of a mile from Atlantic Ave which is filled with touristy-styled gift shops, eateries and cafés. The town is small, but affluent and has a rather large cultural center. I was worried about adding a museum, but after researching several small New England towns like Concord, I realized they had invested quite a bit on cultural infrastructure. There are museums, a large boarding school with a beautiful campus, a theater and numerous private and public schools. Touring Concord allowed me to relinquish my anxiety and create a thriving town.

Adding numerous businesses will also enable you to incorporate more people into your story and give you different storylines to work with.

For example, in *A Garden to Die For*, Michael visits Rosemary's Greenhouse to learn about taking care of a kudzu infestation. In *A Mummy to Die For*, he's able to use Rosemary's Greenhouse as a resource when he has questions about poisonous plants. (Doesn't everyone?) I also introduced a museum in *A Mummy to Die For* so I could host an ancient Egyptian artifact exhibit.

Other businesses you can incorporate into your story are storage units, rental car agencies, private airstrips, UPS stores, restaurants, cafés and bars. By the way, that's the magic of worldbuilding. If you need something, you can create it, within reason.

Rental car agencies are wonderful. If you have a suspect who is driving a rental car, there are diagnostic tools that enable you to find out where the car was driven and when. Most people don't know that if you sync your phone with your rental car using Bluetooth, you could be at risk of identity theft. Major car rental companies have no policies to delete sensitive information.

What type of information is stored when you connect your phone to the car? GPS history, device name, address book, in-car internet search history, music streaming, Wi-Fi identifiers, call log and text messages if you use hands-free calling. My amateur sleuth, Michael, used this information to help nail a suspect. By the way, to protect yourself, make sure you take a few minutes to delete your information if you rent a car.

EXAMPLES OF PUBLIC PLACES IN A COMMUNITY

Airport	Grocery Store	Real Estate Office
Bakery	Gym	Restaurant
Bank	Hotel	Rental Car Agency
Bar	Home & Garden Store	Salon
Bookstore	Hospital	School
Café	Library	Shopping Mall
Church	Museum	Supermarket
Fire Department	Park	Tavern
Floral Shop	Police Department	Town Hall
Gas Station	Post Office	Train Station

The more thriving your community the more opportunities you'll have to create new plots.

Other things to consider:

❈ What road does your protagonist live on? Are there any specific landmarks that need to be mentioned?

❈ Does the protagonist have neighbors? Are they involved in the story? Are they nosey? Good friends?

❈ How does the protagonist get around? Do they have a car? Scooter? Bicycle? Public Transportation? Subway? Train?

❈ Where does your protagonist work? Are they retired? What is their routine? Do they go to the same place every morning to get coffee?

Once you have your community and your amateur sleuth worked out, then you will have established the who and the where! Now you'll have a strong foundation to work from.

Again, don't worry about establishing your entire community right away. You can slowly fill in your community map as you grow your series. Keep your map and add street names, description of houses and businesses. You'll need these to keep continuity of each story.

SURROUNDINGS

Now that you've established the place, you'll need to take into account that it's Christmastime and everything that comes with it.

If you're setting the story in a real city or town, make sure you make the scenes as accurate as possible. If you've never been to that city, you'll need to research enough to make your story believable. If you want opinions about a place but cannot find it on Google, try the Reddit website or TripAdvisor.

I've received immediate responses from Reddit users in the past. People are eager to answer any questions you may have, especially if it's about a place they live in or have visited. You may even let them know that you're researching for a book, and you can add them in the acknowledgements section—this would definitely get people excited about being in a book. Once you've established the place, here are some things you'll need to consider (We'll focus on winter for the examples, since this is a Christmas murder mystery).

- ❀ **WEATHER** What are the highest and lowest temperatures? Does it rain? Snow? Is it dry and sunny? A quick Google search will answer these questions.
  - ➤ **SUNRISE/SUNSET** At what time does the sun rise and set? In Boston, during December, it starts to set between 4:11 PM to 4:21 PM. I found this information at: timeanddate.com/sun/
  - ➤ **OUTSIDE** What does it look like if you're outside? Are most of the trees bare? Is there snow covering them? Is the town surrounded with pine trees? Have the streets been plowed? Can you see the dry grass? What colors do you see?
  - ➤ **HAZARDOUS CONDITIONS** Is there a blizzard? Hail or sleet? Heavy rain? Icy roads? Bridges freezing over? Freezing rain? Strong winds? A lot of authors will use weather events like blizzards or a bridge being out to trap people in a town or hotel.

  "Sorry, the only bridge out of Wilberton has collapsed. It's gonna take several days to figure something out."

  - ➤ **OUTFITS** What are the people wearing? During the day? During the night? Hats? Scarves? Puffy Coats? Gloves? Mittens?
- ❀ **DECORATIONS** How are the houses and buildings decorated? Some may not care much for Christmas, while others may go overboard. The sleuth may have a neighbor that goes all out like Clark Griswold in *National Lampoon's Christmas Vacation*. This

could make for some very funny scenes. Neighbors competing at Christmas can be quite humorous.

❧ **ACTIVITIES** Are there any Christmas parades, shows or festivals in town? Perhaps a business throws a Christmas party every year? In Concord, they have a beautiful manger display with live actors and animals.

❧ **SENSES** What do the townspeople smell when they walk down the streets? Do they stop by a bakery to have a taste of their for-a-limited-time-only eggnog cookies and peppermint mocha? Is there Christmas music playing inside the shops and cafés? Are there Christmas Carolers? Is there a Salvation Army Santa ringing his bell?

These are just a few examples to think about when you're writing about the environment your sleuth is in. Next, let's talk about two of my favorite topics, *murder* and *mayhem*.

Chapter 4
Murder and Mayhem

SETTING UP THE MURDER

Most readers like the murder to be within the first third of the book. (I'm not judging you.) Addressing the murder early does the following:

1. Propels the story forward.
2. Introduces the role of the amateur sleuth and conveys how they will be involved in the murder.
3. Engages your reader. Your audience is no longer a passive observer, they are able to take an active role in working through clues and trying to solve the murder.

Readers will tell you, one of the most enjoyable parts of reading cozy mysteries is working alongside the amateur sleuth, analyzing the clues and trying to solve the mystery. The quicker you are able to do that, the better.

So, without further ado, let's commit murder! (Again, festively.)

WHO IS THE MURDERER?

The murderer needs to be well-developed and their motive for killing meaningful. This person isn't just killing randomly, there is a *reason*, there is intent behind their actions. As we create the murderer together, begin to think about motive.

❀ Why would they kill another human being?
❀ Why were they led to take such *extreme* actions?
❀ Was there no other alternative?

If you already have a murderer in mind, write some of your ideas before we go any further. You can download the murder chart at christmascozymystery.com/resources.

_____

_____

_____

HOW WAS THE VICTIM MURDERED?

This is a great chance to be creative and unique. You want your idea to be original. Let your imagination run wild.

- Was their dental floss soaked in cyanide?
- Were they stabbed with an icicle?
- Bludgeoned with a giant candy cane?
- Pushed from their balcony at a Christmas party?
- Was Santa's pipe tobacco poisoned?
- Were they strangled with their new Christmas scarf?
- Did someone hack their pacemaker via Bluetooth?

You can use weapons, you can use ordinary household objects, you can use poisons. However, if you do use a poison, do your research. You don't need to go into too much detail, but you do need a basic knowledge of a few things, such as:

- Does the poison act instantly?
- What's the timetable between ingestion and death?
- Is it dispensed in a liquid form or powder?
- Can you put it in a drink? Does it dissolve quickly or have a taste to it?

Some poisons take effect instantly, while others mirror indigestion and severe pain before killing the victim. I've included some wonderful resources for poisons.

- *Deadly Doses: A Writer's Guide to Poisons* by Serita Deborah Stevens and Anne Klarner
- *Plants That Kill: A Natural History of the World's Most Poisonous Plants* by Elizabeth A. Dauncey and Sonny Larsson

The following webpage has a list of poisons used by Agatha Christie in her books. I know, there's a typo, but the link works.

owlcation.com/humanities/The-Poisons-of-Agatha-Christe

These links are provided at christmascozymystery.com/resources.

_____

_____

_____

_____

WHERE WAS THE VICTIM MURDERED?

❀ In a house?
❀ In a store?
❀ At a wedding or a funeral?
❀ Were they drowned?
❀ Were they found in a secluded area of the woods by a hiker?
❀ Were there any witnesses?

_____

_____

_____

WHY WAS THE MURDER COMMITTED?

- Why this victim?
- Why now?
- Did they know something or see something they shouldn't have?
- Wrong place at the wrong time?
- Were they going to reveal information that could be harmful to the murderer?
- Were they caught in the act?

A common reoccurring theme in cozies is jealousy. Jealousy doesn't have to be about a woman and a man, it can be professional jealousy. Another is based on fear. They are frightened that the victim is going to reveal something that would ruin their life. Maybe they have a secret past, and the other person is going to reveal it.

Another common plot line is where a couple falls in love. They are both married to a partner that they do not love. So, they work together to kill the other's spouse, therefore, having an alibi when it comes to their spouses' deaths.

_____

_____

_____

_____

_____

_____

_____

_____

Ideas of how to murder someone are everywhere, if you watch for that sort of thing. Recently while at the gym, a young man decided to try and bench press a barbell filled with over two hundred pounds of weight. He lifted the bar from the rack, and it immediately dropped to his chest with a thud, knocking the wind out of him. A trainer and I raced over to help him as he wriggled like a fish to try and get the bar off his chest. Instantly, my mind went to murder.

PLOTTING A MURDER

Let's create a murder together. Here's a storyline you can use based on the weightlifting incident.

Location: Sugar Cove, Florida

Joel is a pompous egomaniac who lives next door to Tim Bland. Tim works hard, and makes a decent living, but nothing compared to his neighbor Joel Richmore. Joel flaunts his wealth and unabashedly flirts with Tim's wife. Tim begins to doubt his self-worth—after all, he can't compare to Joel, and now, he and his wife bicker more and more.

Tim is surprised when Joel shows up at his door and offers him a membership to an invitation-only golf club. "I figured I'd do something nice for Christmas. I've been feeling like a real grinch lately," smiles Joel.

Tim can't believe this is happening. Ever since moving to Sugar Cove, he's been salivating over the private golf course. He grew up playing in golf tournaments with his father and grandfather. A row of framed photos of him as a child on the golf course with his dad line a shelf in his home office.

Joel explains to Tim how the club works. He gives him a two-week probationary pass. It gives the club a chance to get to know Tim, and then the board will vote to see if he's allowed to become a sponsored member. Every chance he gets, Tim goes to the club to play a few rounds. Tim's wife has never seen him so happy. Maybe Joel and Tim will become friends.

It's the day before Tim's two-week guest pass ends. Joel drives up in his golf cart with a friend to where Tim is just about to tee off. He lets Tim know they will be voting that night for new members. He winks at Tim and gives him a thumbs-up.

Tim smiles and thanks Joel. *Maybe I've been wrong about this guy.*

Tim is beside himself. He's going to become a member thanks to Joel. Tim is in the locker room when he overhears one of the men talking about how Joel is having an affair with some poor sap's wife, while the husband spends all his time at the golf club.

"Again?" laughs the other guy. "It's his go-to move."

Tim stops by an Italian restaurant and picks up a lasagna and caprese salad. He runs into a small boutique wine shop and grabs some brie cheese and a merlot. His wife is surprised, and they have a wonderful dinner together. After dinner, Tim asks if she wants to watch a movie. The remote has slipped between the sofa cushions. When he lifts the cushion, he notices a cufflink with a curvy gold *J* beneath the cushion.

His mind immediately goes back to the conversation in the locker room about Joel. His wife seems unruffled and assures him that it must have fallen off of one of the guests from the Christmas party or Thanksgiving feast from a few weeks ago. She promises she'll send out an email blast to everyone that attended to see who lost it. Tim wants to believe her. Maybe what he heard in the locker room was just gossip or about another couple.

Tim's restless. He can't focus on the movie. It was the night that they choose who will be voted in. Joel had assured him that he would be a shoo-in.

Back at the clubhouse, the members meet. When it comes time to vote for Tim, Joel raises an objection about him. He lists several false reasons why he should not be considered a candidate. Tim's membership is denied. Several members share looks of disapproval, but no one wants to get on Joel's bad side.

The next day, Tim drives to the club, excited that his life is finally turning around. A young man at the front desk hands him an official looking envelope as he enters the club. Tim thanks him, assuming that it's his welcome letter. He opens the letter only to learn that his membership is denied. Tim folds the letter and puts it in his pocket. The young man at the counter tells him that his pass expires in one day.

Tim feels gutted. He's consumed by emotion. *What did I do wrong?* He goes out to the driving range with a bucket of balls. Joel pulls up in his personal golf cart. He gets out and pats Tim's shoulder.

"Hey buddy, I heard what happened. I guess someone voted against you."

The other man in the golf cart, snickers and looks away.

"I guess you're not Sugar Cove quality. Sorry about that."

Tim fought the urge to bludgeon Joel with his golf club.

Joel pats him on the back, tips over his bucket of balls, hops onto his golf cart and drives off with his friend laughing.

Tim drops to his hands and knees, picking up the golf balls while other members look on. He drops the half-empty bucket of balls off at the pro-shop and decides to go to the club bar for one last drink, or two.

He shakes his head as he pulls up a barstool. *How could someone be so evil? What did he ever do to Joel?* Tim orders an old fashioned, then another, and then another. His hatred for Joel growing stronger with each drink.

He opens up to the bartender and tells him what happened. The bartender feels sorry for Tim—he seems like a nice enough guy. He tells Tim that Joel is a snake, and that he's destroyed several people's lives. He's a swindler and he's broken up multiple families by cheating with their wives. He tells Tim that it's probably better that he isn't a member, he won't be in Joel's crosshairs.

Tim thanks the bartender and gives him a sizeable tip. He's right. Joel would have just made his life miserable. *First thing I'm going to do when I get home is build a giant privacy fence.*

Tim heads to the locker room to collect his belongings. On the way, he sees Joel lifting weights. A surge of hate rushes through him but he continues toward the locker room. He notices Joel's locker is partially open. He looks around, making sure he is alone, and pulls it open. There's a suit jacket and a dress shirt. He pulls the sleeve toward him, and there it is, a cufflink just like the one he found beneath the cushion.

Tim closes the locker door and makes his way to the gym. Joel is on the bench press. He has a sizeable amount of weight on the barbell. Tim walks over and tells him that he's about to head out. He thanks Joel for trying to help him. Joel gives him a 'whatever' look.

"Hey, before you go, give me a lift-off, will you?"

Tim hesitates, and then helps Joel lift the bar out of the holder. For a moment, he is tempted to shove the barbell onto Joel's throat, but he hurries to the door before he does something horrible. As the door to the gym slams shut behind him, he thanks the bartender again. He was right. He dodged a bullet. He'll build his privacy fence and try to rebuild his life with his wife.

What Tim doesn't see or hear is the bar crashing down onto Joel's windpipe, killing him almost instantly. The video camera outside the gym catches Tim rushing out.

EXERCISE

You can download and print this exercise at the following website: christmascozymystery.com/resources.

Let's break down the key components.

Who is the protagonist?

_____

How would you describe him?

_____

_____

_____

_____

Where is he? Where does he live? Where does he work?

_____

_____

_____

What is the conflict?

_____

_____

_____

_____

Who was murdered? In this story, we realize Joel wasn't actually murdered (or was he?), but Tim is going to be charged. So, who do the police believe was the murderer?

_____

_____

_____

_____

What compelling evidence do the police have that Tim murdered Joel?

_____

_____

_____

_____

What are some back stories we can add? What are unanswered questions? What about Tim's wife, what is unresolved there?

_____

_____

_____

_____

How will Tim clear his name?

_____

_____

_____

_____

_____

What can you add to the story? What other deep dark secrets might Joel have? What about his friend in the golf cart? Maybe that friend in the golf cart gave Joel a little something that caused him to have a heart attack, or become dizzy, unable to control the weights. Maybe Tim sneaks into Joel's house and finds a dirty little secret, a little so-called black book containing pictures of different golf club members' wives. Or vice versa, what if Joel was setting up special arrangements for some of his buddies, but in the end, using them to blackmail them? What if Tim's wife figured that Tim didn't believe her about the cufflink, and found an opportunity to get rid of Joel when she went to the gym looking for her husband?

_____

_____

_____

_____

_____

How is the story resolved? Is it found to be an accident? Did Joel's friend try to kill him? Did the bartender slip him a little something? What really happened? Did the video camera backup suddenly get erased while one of the board members secretly killed Joel? Perhaps Joel had slept with one of the men's wives and had destroyed his life.

_____

_____

_____

_____

Tim can't be alone in this story—what secondary characters can you add? Who does Tim talk to beside his wife? Friends at work? A buddy he meets for lunch?

_____

_____

_____

_____

What does the end of the story look like? Was Tim's wife lying? How does Tim's life return to normal? Who is the murderer? How are they caught? What is their motive?

_____

_____

_____

_____

Basic summary of the ending: Joel is dead. Tim's fingerprints are on his locker, on the gym door and on the barbell. Everyone knows how angry Tim was at Joel. Suddenly, Tim is the number one murder suspect. He has to clear his name.

Think of all the people Tim spoke with. Think of all the people who would point fingers at Tim and say he did it:

❀ The guy at the front desk who handed him the letter
❀ The bartender
❀ Joel's friends
❀ The committee members who voted against him
❀ His wife

What do you think Tim's wife would say? Was she really having an affair? What if Joel had purposely left a cufflink there to mess with Tim's head, to plant the seed in Tim's head that his wife was having an affair?

Now you have a story with legs. You have a wonderful setting. You have a great protagonist. You have conflict. You have a protagonist that has to prove his innocence. That's a pretty compelling reason to get involved in the case.

I hope the story got your mind going. Now let's move on to something even more fun.

PLOTTING MULTIPLE MURDERS

I never thought that I would say this, but multiple murders are a good thing. They're also commonplace in cozy mysteries. If your story is beginning to feel like it's plodding along, kill another person.

NOTE When a story slows and becomes bogged down, it's affectionately referred to as the muddle in the middle.

There are numerous ways to incorporate multiple murders in your book. I'll be naming a few.

Mistaken Identity

Oops, you killed the wrong person example.

> "But she had a key to the door, and she was cleaning the house," Bruce explained.

> "That's her sister, you idiot! She's visiting from Chicago. You killed her sister!"

> "But in my defense, she was wearing socks with sandals."

> "I see," the old man nodded sagely. "Then you have my blessing."

Someone Discovered the Murderer

The killer is found out and they must kill to protect their identity.

Betray Accomplice

There were two murderers, and one of them decides to betray his partner.

Whatever the reason, multiple murders can help you build your suspect list and add twists and turns to your plot.

THE PROTAGONIST'S ROLE

Why is the protagonist compelled to become involved? Again, you are left with dozens of options.

❀ In the story with Tim, he had to become involved because he was the primary suspect in Joel's murder.

❀ Another common way for the amateur sleuth to become involved is a request from a friend or acquaintance. Maybe the crime is of a sensitive nature and can't be handled by the police because it will reveal something from the past.

❀ Perhaps your protagonist saw something that is contrary to what the police are saying. They ruled the death as an accident, when the protagonist knows that something more sinister is afoot.

❀ Maybe your neighbor was murdered. You noticed they had been acting suspiciously lately, like sneaking glances through their curtains, or constantly looking over their shoulder. You've noticed a new car in the neighborhood that you hadn't seen before.

❀ Perhaps someone wrote a suicide note, but you know for a fact that the person wasn't unhappy. Matter of fact, they were ecstatic—they'd just secured a loan from the bank to open a cupcake shop on Main Street and had just finished renovations.

Whatever type of murder scenario you choose, make sure that the investigation merits the time and involvement of your protagonist. Again, this should be through some kind of personal connection.

ACCESSIBILITY TO CRIME SCENE

How does the sleuth get access to the murder scene? This is a great question to think about. First, you have to decide where the murder will occur. Then, decide how difficult you want to make it for your amateur sleuth to access the crime scene.

- ❧ Is it a small town and the protagonist has a friend on the police force?
- ❧ Are they going to pick a lock and sneak in to find more clues? (This is a chance for a little humor. They could Google or perhaps watch a YouTube video on how to pick a lock. Embrace their struggle!)
- ❧ Does the murder occur in their store or office?
- ❧ Does the protagonist find the body and before the police arrive, engage in a little snooping? (Amateur sleuths call this investigating.)

You'll need to find a reasonable way for the sleuth to be able to investigate without setting up too many barriers.

EXAMPLE

The neighbor example is a good one.

> Millie is excited about opening her new cupcake shop. She bought a small building on Main Street and renovated it. She had a beautiful website built and she's been talking about her journey of opening the cupcake store on Facebook and Instagram for months. Her business partner finds her slumped over the desk in her office. A suicide letter saying that it was too much to handle, and that she'd been struggling with depression.

The amateur sleuth could be a good friend who knows that Millie wasn't depressed. The local police insist there was no foul play, that this was a suicide. They say that she was seen at the pharmacy getting pills for depression. The protagonist is sure that Millie wouldn't kill herself and decides to get involved. Oddly enough, some of the Facebook posts about her journey have suddenly disappeared! Who else had access to her personal account? Was someone trying to hide something?

No matter what you decide, you have to give your sleuth access to the crime scene, legally or illegally. In many of my books, my sleuths break a few laws to get information. You've got to decide what barriers you want to create, and how your sleuth will creatively overcome them.

You can find the Protagonist Motivation for Investigating the Murder document at christmascozymystery.com/resources.

Chapter 5
Creating an Outline

TYPES OF OUTLINES

I'm in a lot of writing groups with a lot of authors. All of them outline differently. Here is a breakdown of different ways authors plan out their books. You won't know which works best for you until you've been writing for a while. You may find that a hybrid of different techniques works best for you.

Chapter by Chapter Outline – The author writes out an outline for each chapter, plotting out the entire book this way.

Detailed Outline – The author doesn't break the book up into chapters but creates a very detailed outline. Many times, authors will break the outline up into three to four parts like a play.

Brief Outline – The basic scope and trajectory of the book is written out, but not detailed. Ideas and concepts are listed and loosely described and will be filled out in more detail as the story evolves.

Four-Act Structure – This is similar to the brief outline, with the exception that your story is divided into four equal parts. The authors plan out the important steps of their story in each act, but they're not committed to each scene.

Pantsers – Authors write by the seat of their pants. They develop the story as they work through it. Many say they let the characters lead them through the story.

Sprinters – Authors like to write at a mad pace for a specific period of time, take a mental breather and then begin writing again. I have several friends that use Facebook live to do sprinting sessions together. It's a great way to hold each other accountable.

I've tried all the above, and I've developed a hybrid system that works best for me. I tend to go overboard when researching. I've seen too many authors get bad reviews when they give incorrect information. Yes, I know you are writing a fiction, but readers can be unforgiving when it comes to mistakes. I just read a book where the author wrote an entire page to the reader, reminding them that the story was fictional and that the author chose to change elements of the story to make it more exciting. (In one of Dan Brown's discussions on writing, he talks about being called out for putting the restrooms on the wrong side of the hallway in the Louvre.)

I investigate every tiny detail to make sure it's correct. I've gone as far as buying zip ties and trying to escape from them. It can be done, but the pain involved was not pleasant. I also purchased Kevlar shoelaces to see if I could saw through zip ties and duct tape. Just to let you know, they can. I kid you not.

I begin by writing a *detailed outline* of the story. If I'm discussing a topic like ancient Egypt and mummies, I will invest forty to eighty hours of research to make sure I get *every little detail correct*. In my book *A Mummy to Die For*, I researched Egyptian history, mummification, poisons, voodoo, 3D Imaging, hieroglyphics, how to break into a hotel room, how to break into a hotel safe, etc.… I include detailed articles and photos in my outline.

Once the outline is written, I use my murder sheet and I work backward from the murder, answering all the important questions: Who was murdered? How were they murdered? Why were they murdered? Who are the suspects? How did they know the victim? You get the picture.

I also create a wall of suspects and important characters. I'll search out actors that remind me of the characters and print pictures of them. I also have a chart of each character along with a bunch of details about them.

If I want to know about Ashley Reid, the publicist, I simply look up, and there's her picture with a paragraph-long bio, taped to my wall. You'll figure out your personal preference, but it will take some time. I'm an extreme outliner. My average outline is around ten thousand words. Again, you will find what works best for you as you hone your writing abilities.

FUN NOTE For one of my books, I had to learn how to hack into a locked computer where I didn't have the password. Frighteningly, I found a step-by-step tutorial on YouTube that actually worked. It took me ten minutes to break into a locked computer and change the admin's username and password. (If this writing gig doesn't work out, I may be available for hacking.)

This is how I usually outline my stories. Other mystery writers like to use the four-act structure, which I believe deserves its own section.

FOUR-ACT STRUCTURE

The four-act structure has been around for many years. There are several movies that use this structure that you may be familiar with.

❀ The Karate Kid (1984)

❀ Up (2009) – One of my favorites!

❀ Rocky (1976)

Script magazine offers a brilliant write-up explaining 'The Four-Act Structure.' I found their analyzation of Rocky extremely educational:

scriptmag.com/features/the-four-act-structure

Why am I discussing movies? Most mysteries are structured like a movie or a play and divided up into acts. The four-act structure will help you organize your story and help with pacing. When writing your story, it's good to keep a key thought in mind, it's not *what* happened but *how*. *How* keeps your mind in a problem-solving mode.

Our question and the readers' question should be 'How do we solve the murder?' We know that there is going to be a murder, and we know that we are going to be told who's murdered, and how they are murdered, but it's up to us to figure out *how* to find the murderer and *how* to solve the crime.

We also know that the amateur sleuth is going to succeed. After all, this is a cozy mystery, and we have certain rules and guidelines that we must follow. We've promised the reader that the protagonist will face seemingly unsurmountable odds, but in the end, will reign triumphant. The enjoyable part of the story is creating the obstacles, the twists and the turns, that all lead to the *how*.

I explain obstacles to my students using the brick wall methodology.

Your amateur sleuth is going along just fine, when they run into a figurative brick wall. How do they solve the brick wall problem?

Do they go over it? Do they go under it? Do they go around it? Do they turn around and try another way? Your book isn't just about *how* the protagonist solves the murder, but *how* they navigate through the myriad of obstacles in their way. That's what makes the story interesting.

In a nutshell, this is the basic formula of a cozy mystery:

We're introduced to the protagonist and their world. A murder occurs, and the protagonist is compelled to figure out who the murderer is. Our intrepid sleuth will meet obstacles, follow clues that are dead ends, be led astray, but in the end, overcome them all. The protagonist will confront the murderer, their life may even be in jeopardy, but in the end, our hero will win. The bad guy will be arrested, justice will prevail, the murderer will be punished, and the town will rejoice. Throw in a couple subplots like a love interest and you've got yourself a cozy.

Let's get to work!

Act I: Introduction

The curtain is pulled aside, the spotlight hits the stage, and we get our first glance into a new world. How will you instantly captivate your audience? What will be your first sentence? What are some of the first things your audience will see?

Instead of telling you this is what you do, I'm going to show you. Act I is supposed to introduce us to the main character, to the supporting cast and the community they inhabit. So, I'm going to jump right in.

I like to begin my books with an opening that immediately sets the mood and catches the reader's attention. Here's a sentence I've been toying with for my new novel.

EXAMPLE 1

Light exploded behind Rachael's eyes. She gasped for breath, fingers tearing at the seatbelt as it cut into her throat. An unwelcome darkness crept in. Hot tears streamed from her eyes, tracing the contours of her face. *I'm sorry, Mama, I won't be home for Christmas.*

Immediately, you know that the victim is a woman. You also know that she's in a car and she's being strangled by her assailant. Lastly, we know that she won't make it home to her mother for Christmas. Instantly, we've hooked the reader. *Who is Rachael? Why is she being murdered? Who is the murderer?* We feel for Rachael, knowing that her last thoughts are about her mother, and the fact that she is apologizing for the disappointment and sadness her mother is about to feel.

Where will your story begin? Remember to give your audience the who and the where.

EXAMPLE 2

I like to start my books with something catchy, but you don't have to. Your book doesn't have to have a dramatic hook, it could also be something that's intriguing.

As the train jumped the track and plummeted toward the river, a sad realization filled my mind before I died: *Here I am, sixteen years old, and I've never kissed a girl.*

EXAMPLE 3

Here's another quick story example you can use to get your creative juices flowing. Feel free to take this idea as your own and run with it!

Greg took a sip of his favorite brandy, feeling the warmth expanding in his chest. Bing Crosby's "White Christmas" set the mood. The horseshoe bar was surrounded by rosy-cheeked patrons, their coats and scarves draped over the back of their high back bar stools.

Greg looked up from his drink across the bar. A woman with raven-black hair met and held his stare. He felt his face flush. He smiled awkwardly, then turned away. It felt strange to have someone notice him again. A blast of cold air rushed into the tavern as a man and woman hurried inside, stomping the snow off their shoes.

Greg's eyes fell to his ring finger. The last traces of a pale band are barely visible. He remembered how he and Lizzy used to walk through that same door, arm in arm, laughing. His throat constricted—it had been eight months since his wife had died in a car wreck, and two since he'd removed his wedding band.

He inhaled deeply and slid his drink closer, watching the pale-gold liquid slosh in the cup, heavy, like his heart. His eyes betrayed him as they chanced another look across the bar, but as fate would have it, the raven-haired woman was gone. He raised the drink to his lips and tossed his head back. The brandy burned his throat. It felt good.

Greg fished his wallet out of his back pocket and threw a twenty on the counter. Just as he turned to leave, he felt a hand on his shoulder. He turned to see the raven-haired woman standing behind him. "Greg Bishop," she said quietly, yet firmly. "We need to talk about your wife's murder."

BREAKDOWN

The third example gives us a myriad of opportunities. Let's see where the storyline could take us. We have our protagonist, and we have a setting. We know the time of year.

We learn that Greg lost his wife in a car wreck, and he's still unsettled and tormented by the past. He's conflicted when he sees a woman who is seemingly interested in him. The story gets interesting when she puts her hand on his shoulder and tells him that they need to talk about his wife's murder.

This is where your creative juices should really start flowing. Immediately, your reader will be asking: *Who is this woman? What does she want to talk to Greg about? How does she know him? How does she know his wife was murdered?*

All this time, Greg's been thinking his wife's car crash was an accident. This is a great beginning—you've got all the main elements for a great mystery.

EXERCISE FOR EXAMPLE 3

Who is the protagonist? What do we know about him?

_____

_____

_____

_____

_____

_____

Where does the story take place? Where is he?

_____

_____

_____

_____

_____

Who was murdered and how?

_____

_____

_____

_____

Why would Greg feel compelled to get involved?

_____

_____

_____

_____

REDESIGN EXAMPLE 3

Let's move the story in a different direction. What if you were writing a Paranormal Christmas Cozy?

Greg gets enough courage to buy the raven-haired woman a drink. He motions the bartender over to ask him what she is drinking. The bartender moves aside, then turns back to Greg.

"There's no one there," Andrew the bartender motions to an empty barstool.

"She was there just a second ago, drinking a martini," insists Greg. "She was sitting right there. Black hair, red jacket, checkered scarf…."

"Buddy, that spot's been—" the color drained from Andrew's face. "One second!"

Andrew hurries across the bar and snatched up his phone. He swipes his finger across the screen. With a shaky hand, he holds his phone so Greg can see the screen.

"That's her," nodded Greg. "Like I said, she was sitting right there."

"It's impossible. That's Mary Eldridge. She was killed two weeks ago."

You could add a little more drama to the scene. Perhaps there's a napkin where she had been supposedly sitting. When Andrew picks up the napkin, he sees the words *help me*, scrawled on it.

You are free to use my examples in this book to create your own stories. Just remember the key elements to include in the opening chapter.

FOOD FOR THOUGHT

I'm including this section on marketing and story development because in the first act, you'll be introducing the protagonist and the world they live in.

I encourage people to have their protagonist run a business or some type of creative entity. Why? Because as you develop your character, you will have tools at your disposal to offer your reader additional goodies.

For example, let's say your protagonist runs a coffee shop. You can fill your story with delectable chocolate recipes. How about this? Write a book of recipes written by your protagonist and give it away for free as a reader magnet when someone joins your newsletter or joins your Facebook group. If you run a Facebook campaign, you could give away the book to people that share your post with their friends. You can write something like the following:

> Sign up for my newsletter and get a free copy of Ellie Bank's book, *Chocolate to Die For.*

Create a Pinterest board and Facebook page with the recipes and other resources. Encourage your readers to post their recipes. Offer them an opportunity to have their recipe in your book!

The popular television show *Castle* executed in-character marketing perfectly. Nathan Fillion played Richard Castle, a bestselling author who teams up with Kate Beckett, a NYC homicide detective.

Castle shadows Kate for an inside look at police procedure and police methodology for solving crimes. He creates Nikki Heat—a somewhat dramatized version of Kate Beckett—as the protagonist of his book.

Here's how the show expanded their fanbase and gained a new audience. The first Nikki Heat book was actually published and available at all major retailers. Simultaneously, the show featured the new book by having Richard Castle do book signings. Sales skyrocketed. They even used Richard Castle in all the marketing pieces as being the author of the books.

How well did this work? Take a look at the following Amazon screenshot. Richard Castle's Nikki Heat books became best sellers, selling millions of copies. The execution was brilliant.

SUPPORTING CAST

With just about every successful book and show, another important element is the development of your supporting cast. You'll want to surround your protagonist with a group of friends that collectively embody a large knowledgebase of information that can be tapped at any time to help with the case. Maybe you'll incorporate a friend who is a forensic science professor, or a language specialist. It's also helpful to have friends that have access to information that the average person doesn't. Perhaps your friend works for the phone company or department of motor vehicles. Help yourself out by writing in characters that can assist your protagonist throughout your story.

Make the characters colorful and multi-layered. Maybe that grumpy old courtesy clerk—who always puts your eggs beneath your canned goods—is a retired judge and still has some contacts in the legal system. Create a strong cast of secondary characters that can help move the story along and support your protagonist.

QUICK RECAP OF THE FIRST ACT

1. Introduction of the protagonist
2. Worldbuilding
3. Supporting cast is introduced
4. Murder
5. Compelling reason for the protagonist to become involved

Act II: Sleuthing

Now that there is a murder and the protagonist is involved, your book should evolve around the investigation. How will you move your protagonist around the stage?

Use the Murder Chart to help: christmascozymystery.com/resources

You can use this chart to help tie everything together. The victim should be in the center. Then you list everyone who is connected to the victim. The murder chart should help you work out the following questions:

❀ How did they know the victim?

❀ What would be their motive to kill the victim?

❀ Do each of the people connected to the victim have some sort of deep dark secret that would compel them to kill the victim?

Try to add four to eight suspects—that's plenty to keep the reader guessing.

Once you've created this chart, then the second act can focus on how the protagonist navigates the murder landscape.

Act II will introduce clues for the protagonist to follow. You'll need to figure out the following:

❀ How does your amateur sleuth discover these clues?

❀ How does your sleuth get access to the suspects to question them? Why would they be willing to talk to the protagonist?

❀ What dark secrets do the suspects have that make them look like they could be the one that murdered the victim?

❀ Who would have benefited most from the victim's death?

I've created a Christmas Murder Mystery for you. Let's work through part of the outline and see how this could be turned into a murder mystery of your own.

A Ho! Ho! Horrible Death!

There's a joyous Christmas party going on at Jane's house. She went all out this year: she hired a caterer, a bartender and a pianist to belt out Christmas tunes. Jane even hired 82-year-old Walter Cringle—Lana Cove's very own Santa Claus—to read *The Night Before Christmas* to the children.

The house is buzzing with activity as guests arrive. There's a crowd of people gathered around the piano singing jingle bells, and a line of people filling their glasses with eggnog and enjoying a myriad of bite-sized delectables.

Jane's cat Marvin is stretched out in front of the fireplace watching the revelers disinterestedly. Things couldn't be better. Jane smiles—she can't believe she's pulled it off. Guest after guest thank her for such an amazing party.

Suddenly, there's a scream from the back of the house. Carol Baxter, hands in the air, rushes into the living room. "He's dead!" she screams. "Santa is dead!"

A throng of people rush down the hallway, crowding in front of the bedroom door.

"Don't touch anything," commands Jane. She's watched enough television crime shows to know that you don't disturb the crime scene. She pushes her way through the crowd. Walter is sprawled on the floor at the foot of the bed. A pool of blood soaking into the carpet above his head like a crimson halo.

Jeanette Miles, an emergency trauma doctor, rushes over, kneeling beside Walter. She places two fingers on his carotid. There is no heartbeat.

Dr. Miles looks up at Jane and shakes her head. "He's dead."

EXERCISE

Analyzing the story so far, did we hit all the parts that need to be addressed?

Who is the protagonist?

_____

What do we know about her world so far?

_____

_____

_____

_____

Who was murdered?

_____

_____

Why would she feel compelled to get involved? (Hint: We'll need to add a little more.)

_____

_____

_____

_____

Let's review our answers together.

So far, we have a probable protagonist, Jane. I'll go into more detail about that in just a bit. We know that she is throwing a Christmas party and has worked hard to create a wonderful experience for her friends. We know that Jane is somewhat well-to-do and connected—after all, the party is being catered, she has a bartender, and she's hired a pianist. Her house is also large enough to have a party.

NOTE It's important to remember that I am *just providing an outline*. If I were writing this as a story, I would have fleshed out the descriptors a lot more. I would have immediately addressed Jane's appearance, and delved deeper into the atmosphere, the sights, sounds and smells of the party.

Notice how I describe Walter's death in a way that isn't dreadfully morbid. We can picture him sprawled on the floor at the foot of the bed. There is blood around his head.

We have a large cast of suspects, and since Jane is friends with many of these people, she'll have access to them later on for questioning. Let's continue with some ideas on how the story could move forward.

Why did Santa die? Perhaps Walter caught the caterer going through people's coat pockets and purses in the guest room. The caterer is on parole and if he's caught stealing again, he'll go to prison for a long time. Perhaps there is a warrant out for him and he's trying to fly under the radar. Or perhaps Santa opened the wrong door and caught Pastor White and Gillian Ross being romantic. They're both married, but there's one small problem, not to each other. Did any of these people kill Walter? Maybe Walter wasn't killed, and it was an accident?

The story continues:

> Jane notices that Walter is sock-footed, with one boot partially on. She also notices that there is hair and blood on the corner of the bedframe. Walter was ancient—he was 82 years old. Was he trying to pull on his boot, lost his balance, fell backward and hit his head? Or did something more nefarious happen? Did Santa get into a tussle? Was he pushed backward?

Let's add to the drama. Let's say that the story takes place in a small town and the local police department is lacking resources, and to top it off, murder investigations are extremely rare.

The ill-equipped investigative team arrives and begin to investigate the crime scene. They determine that Walter had been in the process of tugging on one of his boots and fell backward.

"Walter was old after all, and seniors fall, a lot," explains Detective Adams, who was running late for his own Christmas party. "No foul play here," announces Detective Adams. "I'm pretty sure Walter lost his balance. Plus, I can tell he's had quite a bit to drink."

The front of Walter's beard is brittle with dried eggnog. Jane remembers Santa filling up a coffee cup to the brim with eggnog. The party's over, and Jane is lying in her bed. She can't stop thinking about Walter. She's not satisfied with the detective's conclusion. Something about the scene of the crime keeps tugging at her brain.

Wait, she thought. She had to see the police photos of the accident scene. *Did Walter have the wrong boot on the wrong foot*? Why would he stand to try and put his boot on? He would have sat on the bed to pull on his boot. Jane feels compelled to begin her own investigation after talking to Detective Adams, who refuses to change the status to a murder.

Here is where you can have a little fun. Jane creates her own little murder board—a whiteboard where she lists her guests' names and begins her investigation. You can do this too!

Immediately some people are ruled out because they arrived after the time of death, or they never left the living room. There were others that were in a fixed location such as the bartender or the pianist.

Jane finds out that she's missing an expensive watch and a pair of diamond earrings. She remembers seeing the caterer coming up the hall but assumed he had just gone to the restroom. She calls his company to talk to him, but they inform her that he never showed back up to work. She calls Detective Adams and tells him her suspicions. She thinks that maybe Walter caught him stealing and the caterer killed him.

The following can be your first try-fail cycle:

The caterer could be caught trying to sell the watch and earrings. He denies killing Walter. He may be a thief, but he isn't a murderer. He insists he simply wanted cash and stuff he could easily sell. The police hold him for theft and parole violation. Jane's Ring security system actually shows the caterer sneaking outside and rummaging through people's cars during Walter's time of death.

The caterer looks guilty, but in the end, isn't. Jane has to start from scratch. She needs to find more clues and to question more suspects.

Jane replays the events of the evening in her mind. Who can she mark off her list of suspects? Who was gathered by the piano? Who was on the sofa? Who was constantly holding a plate of food, and going back for seconds and thirds?

She begins to cull together a group of suspects. Several of the seniors are eliminated because they couldn't fight their way out of a wet paper bag. Someone at the party is a murderer. Jane begins to dig deeper into motive.

She breaks into Walter's office to see if she can find some clues. She presses a button on his voicemail. There's a message from Tom—his boss at the mall where Walter works as a Santa—letting him know that he has a check waiting for him. And then came a very angry message from an unlisted number, telling him, "This isn't over, Walter. I'm going to destroy you."

Jane doesn't need to know the telephone number, but she recognizes the angry voice—it's Peter Gates, the big condo developer. She saw in the newspaper that Walter had convinced the board to vote against his new development project. Peter would have made millions. Jane makes arrangements to dig deeper into Peter's story.

It's 3 a.m. Jane's security system alerts her that someone or something is outside. She grabs her phone and navigates to the app to watch the live video feed. Suddenly, there's a blinding flash of light and the video goes black. She pads across the cold floor and peeks out the window. She doesn't see anyone.

She grabs a baseball bat from the utility room, sneaks out the back door, and creeps around her garage. No one is there, but her tires have been slashed. She crosses the yard to the front of her house. A large rock lays on the porch beneath the crushed security camera. A note beneath the rock says, *Back off, or you're next.*

Act II ends here and propels you into Act III. Let's review what's happened so far.

Jane doesn't agree with the police's conclusion that the murder was an accident. She begins investigating on her own. *This is a perfect time in the story to bring in a sidekick, someone she can bounce ideas off of—someone that could bring some helpful elements to the investigation.*

Jane follows up on a clue—she suspects the caterer, but in the end, the caterer is not responsible for the murder. Even though the caterer isn't guilty, it doesn't mean that he cannot be utilized in your story. The caterer was constantly moving around the party and serving people. He could have seen something suspicious, and if the police promise to let the DA know that he cooperated with them in exchange of a lighter sentence, he would reveal what he saw.

Jane works through the guest list to narrow down the suspects. She gets access to Walter's home and hears an angry voicemail from Peter Gates. Jane decides that Peter has motive to kill Walter because he's costing Peter *millions* by not allowing him to build a massive oceanfront condo.

Jane goes to bed and is awakened in the middle of the night. When she investigates, an interloper has broken her security camera, slashed her tires and left a note telling her to either stop her investigation, or she's next. You can turn that section of the story into a heart-thumping scene where the reader doesn't know if she is about to come face to face with the murderer—as she climbs the steps to her porch, have a cat scurry out of the bushes.

Jane has a decision to make. Does she continue with the investigation? Or does she pay heed to the warning? You and I both know the answer to that. We deliver a lot of information and excitement in Act II. We close with a heart-pounding scene. This leads us into Act III.

Act III: Dilemmas

We enter Act III with the stakes high. Jane's life is threatened, and one of her party attendees is a murderer. (Oh, another name for the story could be, *A Killer Christmas Party*.)

> There are rumors about Pastor White and Gillian Ross being seen together. Mrs. Ross's husband has been traveling a lot lately, and the pastor has been paying her a little too much attention.
>
> Jane replays the party over in her mind. She remembered seeing them looking quite cozy on the two-seater by the piano at the party. But then, she remembered seeing her sitting alone, and then two children on the small sofa.
>
> Jane asks a couple of her friends, and they say they remembered seeing Gillian leave shortly before Santa was found. Amy—one of the attendees at the party—tells Jane off the record that Pastor White was heavy into the eggnog after they found Walter. She also tells Jane that he was seven years sober and in the same AA group with her—his behavior was definitely suspicious.
>
> Jane also remembers seeing Peter Gates at the party, he was schmoozing with several of the people from the town board. She remembered he double dipped into the eggnog, and then gave her a sickeningly sweet smile.

So, a web is being spun—now we have three suspects. We have the pastor, Gillian and Peter Gates.

EXERCISE

Why would Peter kill Walter?

_____

_____

_____

Why would Pastor White kill Walter?

_____

_____

_____

Why would Gillian kill Walter?

_____

_____

_____

Who had the strongest motive? Who would get the most out of killing Walter?

_____

_____

_____

_____

_____

Peter is motivated by money and greed. Pastor White could lose his wife, his church, his living, everything. Gillian would lose her husband and be an outcast in her community.

Who would threaten Jane? Someone desperate. Someone with enough knowledge to know that Jane was getting closer to the murderer. What can you do to intensify things? Perhaps Jane is pushed down a set of stairs, or nearly sideswiped by a car.

How is their sidekick helping? How are they involved in the investigation?

Actions need to occur that propel the story forward but also bring us closer to the actual murderer.

Act IV: Narrowing Down the Suspect List and Conclusion

All the pieces are coming together. Jane and her sidekick confront Peter with the voicemail. He acknowledges that he left the voicemail, but he would never kill Walter. Jane talks to several people at the party, and they confirm that he was too busy trying to woo the town council to see things his way, that he didn't have an opportunity to commit the murder.

It's late, Jane is exhausted. She gets in the shower and closes her eyes, letting the steam envelop her. When she gets out of the shower, she sees that she has a voicemail, and several texts.

She listens to the voicemail—it's Gillian. She says she has important information and needs to talk to her in person immediately. The texts say the same thing. Gillian doesn't feel safe and there's something urgent she needs to tell her before it's too late. Jane texts Gillian and tells her to come over. She throws on some clothes and puts a pot on the stove, boiling water, to make tea for her and Gillian.

Ten minutes later, there's a knock at the door. Jane hurries out of the kitchen and peeks out her front window. She sees Gillian's car and Gillian in her fur jacket, a wool hat and boots. Jane unlocks the door and opens it slowly, only it's not Gillian, it's Pastor White wearing a fur coat and a wig. He shoves the door open and slams Jane against the wall. He smiles and brandishes and evil-looking knife.

Jane confronts him, tells him he's being crazy, that Walter's death was an accident, but Pastor White isn't listening. She runs through the living room, grabs a lamp off the table and hurls it at the minister. The lamp hits him in the forearm, shattering. He grabs her arm as she rounds the corner and wrenches it up behind her.

She yelps in pain and lashes out hard, driving the heel of her foot into his knee. He's stunned for a second, Jane feels his grip loosen. She breaks free, rushes across the kitchen, throwing herself against the stove, she grabs the pot by the handle and throws the scalding water at the minister.

He howls in pain and drops to the floor. One more bonk to the head with the pot, and he's out cold. She calls the police and rescue squad. It's a small town—within five minutes, the police and rescue squad arrive. The murder is solved.

But what happened to Gillian? Jane calls Gillian's number, she hears the phone ring. It's inside the preacher's jacket pocket. Jane tells the police about Gillian—they try to question the pastor, but he's in agony and not talking. They dispatch officers to Gillian's house. Would the pastor risk taking Gillian to his house? She digs in his pocket and finds his keys. She runs outside, pops the trunk. Gillian is bound, gagged and freezing in the trunk. She's safe.

The Pastor is arrested for murder, attempted murder and kidnapping and will go to prison for many, many years. Gillian is brought in for questioning. She wanted to tell everyone about what the pastor had done, but he threatened to kill her, just like he had done to Walter. He had told her that everything would blow over, that the police had decided that it was an accidental death—if only Jane wouldn't have gotten involved. In the end, we find out that Pastor White shoved Walter in a heated argument. Walter hit his head and died instantly. In a panic, Pastor White arranged the boots to look like he was trying to pull them on and fled the room. Unfortunately for him, amateur sleuth Jane was on the case, and took him down.

By time you reach the end of the story, you will want to have accomplished the following:

❧ You'll want to make sure that you've tied up all the subplots.

❧ You'll want to make sure that Pastor White is going to be punished for his crimes.

❧ You'll want the town to return to normal. In this case, as normal as it can be. Poor Walter will be dearly missed.

❧ Now that Jane has been bitten by the amateur sleuth bug, we'll want to see how she evolves into a small-town crime investigator. Your readers will be interested in learning more about Jane and her escapades, so this would be a good time to sprinkle in any hints to a sequel.

There are some subplots that you should continue and let them age like fine wine. Most of the time, subplots are built around romance. Some scenarios are:

- She likes him, but either she or he is just getting out of a relationship and needs some space.
- She or he is already in a relationship.
- She likes him, and he likes her, but they are taking their time.
- Maybe in this case, a local reporter is impressed with Jane's moxie and asks her out to dinner for a private interview.

There can also be other plots percolating in the background. Perhaps it's not over with the town board and Peter. He may not be a murderer, but he could still be a conniving jerk. What is he up to?

What about the cat that jumped out of the bushes and scared her? Maybe the cat is a stray and Jane decides she would like the companionship of a four-legged friend. Cozy readers love pets.

Again, this is *your* world. Let your imagination fly and have fun. Create friends that you would love to have. Give your character a sense of spontaneity and spunkiness that you wish you had. Live vicariously through your character!

If you're writing a *paranormal* Christmas cozy, your witch could have a mouse as a familiar. She could decorate the little mouse hole with a wreath and hang a little stocking filled with cheese above it. Cheesy (no pun intended) but cute.

In the middle grade *Myrtle Hardcastle* series, the cat plays an important role in the murders, adding much needed lighthearted moments. A word of caution, once you've introduced a pet, and readers fall in love with that pet, don't let anything happen to it. Bestselling author James Patterson joked about his fans writing to him, warning him that he better not let anything happen to his protagonist's dog.

In paranormal cozy mysteries, you'll see cats, dogs, rats, birds, among others, as the protagonist's familiars. In paranormal cozies, most of the animals can speak or engage in some type of conversation with their masters. In my *Merry and Moody Cozy Witch Mysteries*, I have a cat named Rufus and a rat named Samuel, who add a lot of humor to my stories. They're always commenting on their human counterparts. Fans of the cozy genre actively search for cozy mysteries with pets. Cats are the favorite, followed by the man's best friend, a dog.

ENDING I like to end my books with the protagonist in a familiar place with their friends. I usually end my books where they are talking over dinner, or coffee and everyone is in high spirits.

If you are writing your book as a series, you may end the book with a hint that there is more to come. Perhaps when Jane goes on the dinner date with the journalist, he can pass on a tidbit of information about something else that needs to be investigated. Keep your options open.

EXAMPLE

I wanted to give you a lot of original ideas to work with. So here is another Christmas murder story. Enjoy!

It's Christmas Eve. Michael Frost wakes up to the sound of someone pounding on his door.

"I'm coming," he rasps.

He sits up and is instantly wide awake. There's a woman in bed with him—a crimson stain covers her torso. He leaps from the bed, crashes to the floor, pulling a lamp and nightstand on top of himself. He untangles himself, gets his knees under him, grasps the mattress and pulls himself up.

"Where am I?" His eyes fall onto the woman again. *Who is she? What's going on*? Questions fill his brain. There's a loud crash from the adjoining room. Police officers flood into the house, guns drawn. A burly, buzz cut officer grabs Michael, slams him against the wall, and cuffs him.

"Wait! Wait! There's been a horrible mistake! I don't know what's happening."

The police officers lead Michael through an unfamiliar apartment. Doors crack open as the occupants watch the police lead a disheveled man to the elevators. "Is that Michael Frost?"

"Where am I? Where are you taking me?"

"You're at the Westmore Apartments, and we're taking you in for questioning."

"But…," Michael fell silent, the Westmore Apartments were for the extremely wealthy. "I want to speak with my attorney."

"No kidding," smirks one of the officers.

They lead Michael through the lobby. The doorman holds open the door and gives him an icy stare. Michael shivers as a blast of arctic air swirls around them, sending an empty beer can scuttling down the sidewalk. The police lead him to an unmarked car. Just as they are about to place Michael in the back, the officer helping him slips on the icy sidewalk and falls, landing hard on his back.

Michael dashes past the other surprised officer and races across the street. A car clips him, but he rolls and leaps to his feet, disappearing between a row of buildings into the night.

DISCUSSION

❧ We've introduced the protagonist, Michael.

❧ We've done some worldbuilding so our readers can imagine the scene. He's in a pricey apartment with a dead woman. He's led down the hallway to an elevator, through the lobby, to a police car. It's nighttime and it's cold and icy.

❧ We've got a murder and instant conflict. Michael is the key suspect in a murder and he's just complicated things by running from the police.

❧ Who is Michael? Who is the woman? How did she get murdered? How did Michael wind up in bed with her? How did the police find out about her?

Let's fill in some information on Michael and where he lives.

Michael Frost runs an eclectic, chic café named *Unfiltered* in a small village named Oak Cove, near Westchester, New York. It's a tiny triangular slice of land—the southern edge is bordered by the Croton River and the Hudson on its west. The streets are filled with dozens of boutique shops and trendy eateries.

Michael is a bit of a local celebrity. He's considered to be one of New York's most talented coffee artisans. His newly published, limited edition, coffee table book *Unfiltered* (Yes, it has the same name as his café) launched to rave reviews, selling out in local bookstores in a single day. His new holiday blend variety pack sold out in minutes. Michael is a rising star in the coffee world. When he's not creating exotic new blends, he likes to take Bixby, his golden retriever, to the local dog park or work on his poetry.

What do the police uncover during their investigation?

Let's make Michael's life a little more difficult. The police have video of Michael entering the hotel and getting onto the elevator with the victim. The police run his financials and find a cash deposit of $10,000 and a charge to a pricey restaurant within walking distance of the Westmore Apartments. Surveillance footage shows Michael and the mystery woman sharing a drink. The CSI team finds a bloody knife with his fingerprints, hidden under the carpet in the closet.

The police ID the dead woman as well-known savage food critic named Mary Christmas. The bad news keeps piling up on Michael. It seems that Mary wrote a scathing review of Michael's café, and it was due to be released Christmas morning.

Now we've got ourselves a story!

Michael has a lot of questions, but he's not going to be able to answer them alone. Michael runs a popular café—a lot of people like him. He needs a supporting cast that he can trust to help him navigate the investigation and prove his innocence.

Maybe Michael has a love interest, or a best friend, or a small group of friends that are willing to help him and provide sanctuary for him as he works through things. He'll need someone to run his business while he's in hiding. Perhaps he has a friend that works for a theater group and is able to help create a disguise for Michael so he can actively work on the case and clear his name.

Michael is fuzzy about the past few hours. He needs to retrace the last twenty-four hours and find out what's going on, and who the real killer is. I'll give you a few suggestions to work through as a backstory, and to explain the events that took place before they found Mary Christmas in bed with Michael.

Backstory.

Mary Christmas is a vengeful woman that believes she is the center of the universe. In the world of food and restaurants in the small but thriving community of Oak Cove and surrounding municipals, she might be right. She's personally brought several restaurants to their knees.

Mary reviews a new French and Italian fusion restaurant that is trying to get on its feet. She decimates the restaurant, saying that their food is unimaginative and tastes like a moldy dishcloth. She goes on to say that she would rather eat a shoe than their slop. The article is filled with pictures she took of her meal. To top things off, she films a video with her phone of a server taking a sip from an overfilled wine glass as he carries the drink from the bar to a table—a clear health code violation.

When confronted by a reporter, George Abbott—the owner of Feu— says the man in the video doesn't even work at his restaurant. He claims that she's being paid off by other restaurants to give them a bad review.

In the end, however, Mary's article and video do their damage. Mary has thousands of followers on Instagram and Facebook. The local news even picks up on the story of the server, showing the employee sipping from the glass of wine over and over again. Just like clockwork, the health inspector shows up at George's restaurant to investigate.

Mary's review, the bad press and the local news do an incredible amount of damage, and George is about to lose everything. He fires most of his staff, leaving him with only a skeleton crew. Patrons to his restaurant have trickled down to a few diners a night. Vendors have canceled contracts with him, not wanting to associate their brand with a sinking ship. And if things couldn't get worse, George sees a story on local coffee superstar, Michael Frost.

"He looks so smug," growls George angrily as he looks out over his empty restaurant. The local news shows a line of patrons waiting to get inside Michael Frost's café. His new book *Unfiltered* splashes up on the screen. The announcer comments people can't get enough of his book.

"You pretentious jerk," George seethes. "I'll take care of you." He slams the T.V. remote on the bar.

Filled with rage, George decides to create an elaborate plot to murder Mary Christmas and put the blame on Michael Frost. George hires Carol—an out-of-work actress—who is desperate for work. He explains the plan to her. She is to disguise herself, so she looks very similar to the critic Mary Christmas. She is then to convince Michael that she is a journalist visiting from the UK on behalf of Roast Magazine, a magazine recognized worldwide by coffee enthusiasts with a readership of nearly two million people. She'll tell him that she would like to talk to him about his new book *Unfiltered* and perhaps do a story on his rebellious exotic blends. After all, he is the bad boy of coffee.

Once George and Carol perfect their plan, she contacts Michael. He instantly agrees to meet her at a local bar where they can talk.

Carol and George have scouted out the bar beforehand and they know where the security cameras are. The actress is dressed up to look like Mary Christmas. She keeps her back to the camera, so the camera doesn't see her face. When Michael's not looking, she puts a drug in his drink. It's not enough to knock him out, just enough to make him a little spacy and to lower his inhibitions.

After a couple drinks, Carol tells Michael that she's set up a green screen and camera equipment back at the apartment she's staying in for the next couple of weeks—she explains that it's one of those Airbnb rentals.

Michael is so excited about a spread in the magazine that he jumps at the opportunity. He grabs an Uber driver for them who takes them to the apartment. They nod to the doorman, get on the elevator, and go to the third floor. She unlocks the door and invites Michael in. She motions him over to the bar where she makes a drink for him—she drugs the drink, full dose.

She excuses herself for a minute. She goes in the restroom, takes off her wig, puts on a pair of glasses, switches her reversible jacket to the other side, and puts on a pair of flats, stuffing everything into her purse. Michael passes out. She exits the apartment, climbs the stairs to the fifth floor, rides the elevator down, and leaves the building.

George appears from the bedroom wearing a pair of gloves and medical shoe covers. He's killed Mary Christmas. He drags Michael into the bedroom. He removes Michael's shoes, pants and shirt. He folds them and puts them on a chair across the bedroom. He half lifts, half drags Michael onto the bed beside Mary Christmas. He takes Michael's right hand and closes his hand around the handle of the knife, and then he hides the knife under the carpet in the closet.

NOTE I was very specific about a couple things so you can later use them as clues. First, I said he folded Michael's clothes and put them on a chair in the corner. Very unlikely, Michael would take the time to fold his clothes. Second, Michael is left-handed, and the fingerprints that are going to be on the knife are right-handed.

George rinses out the wine glass with the drugged wine in it and refills it with regular wine. The evidence will show that Michael killed Mary Christmas. The video evidence from the local pub and the elevator will show him with Mary Christmas, entering the apartment proper, walking through the lobby and entering the elevator. Only we know that it is the actress.

George is ecstatic. The police will come in and arrest Michael. Mary Christmas is dead, and that smug jerk Michael will be rotting in jail.

This should be a fun story for you to work through. Once you've worked through your story and created your first manuscript, you will need to have it edited. I'm going to share with you my editing process and then my beta reader process. I realize it may be a few months before you are ready to begin editing, but I want to make sure you have the necessary information. Happy writing!

Chapter 6
Writing, Editing, Rewriting, Revision and All That Fun Stuff

WRITING WORKDAY

How many words do I write a day? You'll need to find what works best for you, and you won't know until you begin. When I first started, I labored over every single sentence, every single word choice—it was a nightmare. I struggled to write five hundred words a day. A thirty-thousand-word book seemed impossible.

Now, nearly a decade later, I write 2,000–3,000 words a day. I am still guilty of going back chapter by chapter and revising, but that is a comfortable number for me. I have friends that pound out 8,000–10,000 words a day. I can't even think or speak that fast. I don't know how they do it, but they do.

So, the math is simple. If you write 500 words a day, and you write every single day, then in a month, you would have 15,000 words. So, a 40,000-word book would take you about three months to write.

I've created two charts for you to use to keep track of your daily writing. The first is an excel spreadsheet with formulas added to it to keep track of how many words you write. The second is a simple grid created for you to pencil in your daily work. You can download the worksheets from christmascozymystery.com/resources.

EDITING

Once I've done all the research and written my mystery, I send it off to one of my editors. Wait, you said *one* of your editors? Yes, I use a couple editors. I use a copy editor who simply focuses on grammar and punctuation, as well as a developmental editor to look for plot holes and continuity problems. Let me explain.

My first version of the story goes off to my *developmental editor*. Their job is to try to poke holes in my story and to find any plot issues. They can also let you know if things are out of sequence or if parts of the story lag. You always want to remember that *every* chapter should propel the story forward or reveal something that's pertinent to character development or to the story.

QUICK NOTE That being said, you don't want your story to be action, action, action. Just like music, there's not a maddening string of notes in quick succession. Songs are broken up into numerous parts. Ben Folds, a famous musician, said he allows his songs to build and build until he knows his listener's ears are ready for a chorus or bridge, and it's a relief because they were ready for that change.

Next time you watch a crime show, pay close attention to the music. Warm playful music teases us along while the protagonist spends time with family or friends. Up-tempo music plays when there is a chase scene, or the protagonist is sneaking up on someone. Your book should have this type of pacing.

Once I receive the manuscript back from my developmental editor, I work on fixing the areas they've pointed out. At times, they may suggest deleting a chapter, or perhaps they'll suggest you have too many suspects or too many characters. There may also be a time when you and your editor will have disagreements. They may say that one of your favorite chapters needs to be removed, that it bogs the story down and doesn't provide any real value. And I must warn you, it will be difficult, and you'll say to yourself, *but it's such an amazing chapter!* Amazing or not, if it doesn't enrich the story, reveal something important or propel the story forward, then your editor may be right.

That's when you need to take a step back and give yourself some time. Maybe the chapter doesn't belong. Maybe the information could be sprinkled throughout the story instead of bringing it to a screeching halt. You'll find out once you have your beta readers go through your manuscript. They'll let you know if the chapter in question sticks out like a sore thumb.

Once I've reworked the story, I send it off to my *copy editor*. My copy editor meticulously works through the manuscript looking for grammatical errors. Their job is to look for: punctuation, tenses, run-on sentences, misspellings, incorrect word usage, repetitive word usage, you get the gist.

Repetitive word usage happens a lot. I was recently reading a book, and it seems the author fell in love with the word *chided* halfway through the manuscript. In one paragraph, I counted the word *chided* six times. (A great resource to use when you struggle to think of another word is Word Hippo. The website is wordhippo.com. It does a phenomenal job providing alternatives.)

Just is another common word that is overused. Just as I turned the corner, I saw Jim. I sprinted through the parking lot, just as he sped off in his car.

I use the AutoCrit software to check for repetition and pacing. You can learn more about the software at autocrit.com.

Unfortunate But True: The more you write and edit, the more critical you will become when reading other author's books. You'll spot every grammatical error and every tiny nuance.

BETA READERS

Once your copy editor has reviewed your manuscript, they'll send it back to you. You'll be able to work through their suggested changes and refuse or accept them. After I work through the story, making all the suggested revisions, then I send my book out to beta readers. This is not my ARC (Advanced Reader Copy) group. This is a group of people in my target audience that I hire to give me feedback. You don't need a paid beta reader of course—there are beta readers who are willing to help for free if you prefer. In my case, most of my beta readers have advanced English degrees or are professors at schools or universities.

I absolutely love this process. The readers I work with provide me with a detailed report focusing on plot holes, pacing, misspellings, grammar, their likes, dislikes, inconsistencies, characterization and motivation, backstory and setting, and worldbuilding.

Once I fix everything that needs to be fixed, my book goes back to the developmental editor for a final readthrough. I again make any necessary changes and then I send the book to my copy editor. The copy editor finds any grammatical mistakes and sends it back to me. After all of this back and forth, I send this final revision to my ARC readers.

ARC READERS

My ARC readers are wonderful. They're brutally honest, and often find that errant comma or misspelling. I use my ARC group to write reviews for Amazon, Barnes & Noble, and Goodreads. If you read cozy mystery reviews, many times you will often see this sentence: "I received a free copy of this book to review." That comment is from an ARC reader. Oftentimes, I'll take their reviews and use it on the cover or back cover of my books. I'll also include snippets of their reviews on my ads.

After going through this extensive process, I usually feel good about releasing my book into the wild.

RECAP

My humble advice to you is don't rely on self-editing. You *will* miss things. I cannot tell you how many instructional books I've read about writing and publishing that are filled with grammatical errors. What do readers hate? They *hate* being completely absorbed in a great story and then suddenly being ripped out because of a misspelling. I was recently reading a Nancy Drew book that was filled with misspellings. In one section, the man she was sitting beside suddenly became a woman. I found myself reading and rereading the paragraph to see if I missed something.

A common theme I see in reviews is the following: "I really wanted to give this book four stars, but the lack of editing is atrocious. I'm only giving it two stars." I put my books through multiple edits and multiple reads for this reason. Reviews like that can knock your sales down to zero in a hurry.

Be Productive!

While your editor is working on your book, you can begin writing your next! Series sell. Plus, if you begin working right away on your second book, your characters, your town, and your supporting cast will all be fresh in your mind.

Chapter 7
The Cover

BOOKS ARE JUDGED BY THEIR COVER

NOTE All images and graphic files are available at the website christmascozymystery.com/resources.

How many times have you purchased a book because of its cover? A good cover can stop a prospective buyer in their tracks. Fortunately, the cozy genre enables you to create fun, colorful, playful covers. Best of all, it's expected.

Quite often, as soon as I have a solid idea and outline worked out for my manuscript, I will begin working with my graphic artist on cover design. I like to hang it on the wall in front of me for inspiration as I write.

Most cozy covers are very similar to chick-lit books. They're known for simple colorful illustrations or vector artwork with catchy titles.

CHICK LIT COVER EXAMPLES

CHRISTMAS COZY MYSTERY EXAMPLES

Cozy mysteries usually have clever titles. For Christmas, you'll see titles like *Twas the Knife Before Christmas, Yule Be Dead* or the *Twelve Slays of Christmas*. I'm going to name the Mary Christmas story example, *Who Killed Mary Christmas*—it's catchy, fun, and interesting.

Most cozy mystery covers are created by layering vector images—however, there are a few authors who like to have their covers professionally illustrated. I'm one of those authors. Ninety-five percent of my covers are original artwork.

WHAT IS A VECTOR IMAGE?

A vector graphic is a computer-made image that is made up of points, lines, and curves that are based on mathematical equations, not pixels. Adobe Illustrator can be used to create vector images.

WHAT ARE ILLUSTRATIONS?

An illustration is any picture drawn by hand or with the assistance of a device like an electronic drawing pad.

Here's an example of an electronic tablet used for digital art.

My graphic artists draw a sketch of the cover first, send it to me for approval, and then they color it in. They tend to use Adobe Photoshop.

VECTORS VS ILLUSTRATIONS

In complete transparency, vector covers are much less expensive than an illustrated cover. Illustrated covers can run you anywhere from $450 to $1,000 and are much more labor intensive. Vector covers can be done for around $100 to $300.

Sometimes I will play around a bit with a design that I like, and then send it to my illustrator to fix it up. For example, for the book *Who Killed Mary Christmas*, I found an image on Shutterstock that I thought would work perfectly for that book. Sites like Shutterstock.com and Pond5.com offer a myriad of images that you can use for your covers. Follow along as I create a simple cover.

'WHO KILLED MARY CHRISTMAS' PROJECT

Step 1

I searched through Shutterstock for a picture of Santa on a rooftop. I found a great picture that I think I'll be able to work with.

Santa Claus Stuck In The Chimney On Snow Roof. Christmas Cartoon Vector Illustration.

By chimeyuserts

Step 2

Using Adobe Illustrator, I removed the words *Merry Christmas and Happy New Year*. If you don't know how to use Illustrator, there are literally hundreds of people at Fiverr.com that will remove elements from a piece of artwork for a few dollars.

Step 3

I played with a few fonts and added them to the cover. I was going for bold and Christmassy. I also added a subtitle to give a little more information as to what the book is about: "From brewing magic, to a death so tragic."

Step 4

I added a moon, and inside the moon I added the words, *For Fans of Castle*. I'll explain in detail why I did that a bit later. I also added my name at the bottom in large print. The snow at the bottom of the image was a perfect place for my name. Here's the cover so far.

Step 5

This is about where my artistic skills end. I think the cover looks pretty good, but I would definitely like it to look a bit more polished. My next step would be to forward the design to my graphic artist, along with the original artwork from Shutterstock.

Step 6

What are some elements that I could add? What should I have my graphic artist address? In one word, *typography*. I would definitely want him to play with the fonts to see if he can find something a little more expressive and Christmassy. Perhaps I could have a little snow on top of the words Mary Christmas. I could change the letter *O* in *WHO* to a wreath. Another idea is to have a few drops of blood beside the chimney. I'll send those ideas to him and let him work his magic.

Step 7

If you want to do the design completely yourself, you do have more options! Fontbundles.net offers dozens of beautiful free fonts. I've used quite a few of them on my book covers.

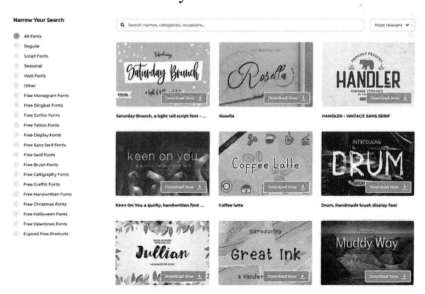

Step 8

Once you are finished with your cover, upload it to Facebook. There are numerous author groups on Facebook that will happily give you feedback on your cover. I do this *every* time I create a new cover, and I *always* receive *invaluable* feedback from other authors.

Step 9

Make the changes and upload your image again. Keep in mind that you want your image to be saved at 300 DPI for quality purposes. If you need help with that, again I suggest Fiverr.com.

One more note, make sure your book cover is legible when Amazon displays it in a thumbnail. Amazon will display your book cover image in multiple sizes. The larger thumbnail is 217 x 320 pixels. The smallest thumbnail size is 103 x 160 pixels. Take your image and resize it to see if you can still read it.

Going into a complete design tutorial is outside the scope of this book, so I'm going to discuss how to work with a graphic designer and how to make sure your final project is exactly what Amazon and your audience wants.

GRAPHIC ARTISTS

I want to hire a graphic designer—how do I do that? How do I find a graphic designer? Finding a great graphic designer can take some work. Over the past seventeen years, I've worked with many artists. I now have four that I have worked with consistently over the past five years, all of which are at the top of their game.

Take your time and research artists. Look at their portfolios and make sure that you ask for examples of work that they've done in your genre or a similar genre. I found most of my artists through 99designs.com. I was also introduced to another artist by an author friend, and I found another graphic designer on Fiverr.

99DESIGNS To be completely transparent, 99designs is expensive. However, if you are creating a new series and you want a tremendous amount of input and design ideas, 99designs is the way to go. If you want an exceptional cover to launch your book, 99designs will create an environment where there are twenty to thirty designers competing to design your cover. You'll get dozens of cover ideas from a lot of creative designers. Again, the cost is quite high, anywhere from $299 for bronze up to $1,199 for platinum. Every contest comes with a money-back guarantee, and you have full copyright and ownership of whatever they design.

FIVERR You may also find quite a few talented graphic artists on Fiverr.com. The cost for Fiverr usually runs from $60–$300 depending on the complexity of the project. If you hire a designer from Fiverr, make sure you check out their portfolio and that they have a significant amount of five-star reviews. Also take a look at what they offer for their prices. Do they offer full commercial use? Do they offer the source files where you can edit the e-book or hard copy files? How many revisions can you make to the cover? Another thing to check is to see how many jobs they have queued up. If they have ten jobs ahead of you, then it could mean that it would be weeks before you get your work done. Make sure the graphic artist has availability to do the work in a timely manner.

FACEBOOK There are literally dozens of private Facebook groups that unite authors with illustrators. As an author, you simply post what you would like designed, and artists will respond to your post. Many of them will immediately share their portfolios or book covers with you that are similar to your description. These groups are also perfect to display your own covers and receive feedback. I've included several groups on our website in the resource section.

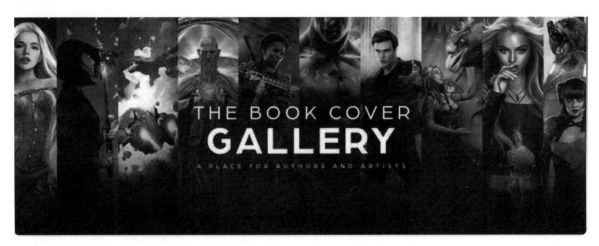

Book Cover Gallery - A Place for Authors and Artists
🔒 Private group · 8.2K members

WORKING WITH GRAPHIC ARTISTS

Once you have hired a graphic artist, you will need to convey your vision of your dream cover to them. Here are the steps that I follow when I work with my illustrator.

Step 1

One of the first things I do when creating a cover from scratch is I provide my graphic artist with covers from my genre that I like. I may include notes like: I like how the man and woman are drawn and their style of clothing. Or I like the color scheme and the way they displayed the title. This gives my artist a general idea of the stylization of the book.

Step 2

I'll pick a scene or two from my book and explain it to them. For example, for my book *A Role to Die For*, I drew a Christmas scene of a couple sitting in a coffee shop. Outside the window of the café, I drew a snowman that had been stabbed. (Who would do such a nefarious deed?) I added some additional elements, footsteps in the snow, decorative streetlights, etc. I sent the picture to my illustrator with additional details. See if you can figure out who drew which.

As you can see, my artistic skills are remedial to say the least. But my artist was able to turn things around and create a beautiful cover. Most of the time, it will take several revisions before your graphic artist nails your cover. Make sure that you agree to multiple revisions and that you own the artwork.

Step 3

I always work closely with my graphic artist to make sure things don't go astray. Andrew, one of my artists, always sends me several quick sketches. Each sketch depicts a different view, or camera angle of the same scene. He gives me detailed explanations as to what is happening in each scene. I decide which one I like, and then he continues working.

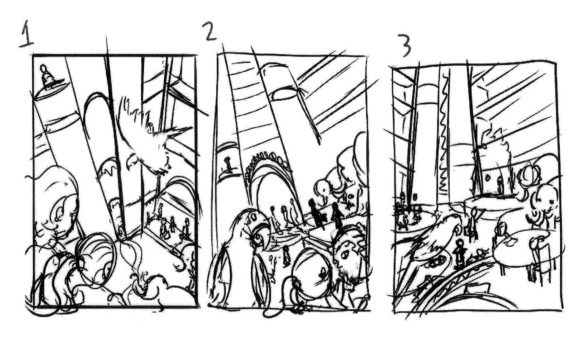

Working closely with your illustrator will save you a lot of time. Make sure they update you on each part of the process.

So remember a few important details:

1. Look for books from a similar genre that have a similar color palette.

2. Sketch out the scene you want to depict on your cover.

3. Send any elements you may want them to use on your cover. For example, for my book *Sleighed*, I needed a large sled being pulled by reindeers. I searched and searched until I found a picture of what I wanted and sent that to my illustrator. Here's the result.

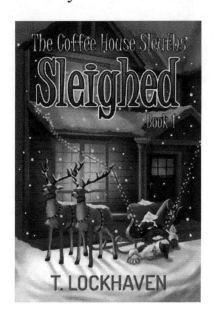

4. Stay in constant communication with your artist. Ask every few days to see updates. You don't want the project to move too far forward if there are mistakes. Make sure the person you hire allows free revisions!

As everything starts moving along, ask yourself these questions:

1. Is the book bright and colorful?

2. Is the title catchy?

3. Will the audience immediately recognize the book as a cozy mystery?

4. Are there elements of the story incorporated in the cover?

5. Are the fonts bold and clearly legible?

Before we move on to working on blurbs and making sure you have quality content, let's see if my working cover for *Who Killed Mary Christmas* hits all the right targets.

1. **Is the book bright and colorful?** Yes, brilliant reds against a dark sky filled with stars, and golden lights glowing from houses. Anyone seeing this book will instantly know that it is a book based at Christmastime. You can take a closer look at the book cover at christmascozymystery.com/resources, under *Images and Graphics*.

2. **Is the title catchy?** Yes, it's a play on words since the victim is named *Mary Christmas*. It also gives us a hint about what the book is about by incorporating the tag line "From brewing magic, to death so tragic."

3. **Will the audience immediately recognize the book as a cozy mystery?** Yes. The cover is vectorized and playful as is expected in the cozy genre. The title and subtitle also give us clues that this is a murder mystery that doesn't take itself too seriously.

4. **Are there elements of the story incorporated in the cover?** Yes. We know from the cover that there is going to be a murder. Not Santa, but there is going to be a murder according to the title and that it is going to occur at Christmastime.

5. **Are the fonts clear and legible?** Not as much as I would like. I would make sure my design guru jumps in and fixes those, so they read clearly no matter the size of the cover.

Even though cozy mysteries generally have very simple covers, it doesn't mean that you don't want them to look professional. I've seen a lot of authors who have simply grabbed stocked images, layered them on top of each other, used Times New Roman as the font and published the book. Then they wonder why their book isn't selling. Simplicity can still look masterful. Here are some examples. You can see the full color display at christmascozymystery.com/resources.

Chapter 8
Pseudonym

CHOOSING AN AUTHOR NAME

Do I need a pen name? A nom de plume? You don't have to have a pen name, but a lot of authors like to keep their private lives *private*. A pen name gives the author a bit of anonymity. Pseudonyms have been used throughout history by some of the most famous authors.

❀ Mark Twain → Samuel Clemens

❀ Dr. Seuss → Theodor Seuss Geisel

❀ Mary Westmacott → Agatha Mary Clarissa Christie—Agatha Christie said that she used a pen name so she could switch genres from mystery and crime to romance.

❀ A. M. Barnard → Louisa May Alcott

Many times, authors will use pen names to hide their gender. Ask J. K. Rowling (real name: Joanne Rowling). Her publisher was worried that pre-teen boys may not accept stories about wizards written by a woman. The middle initial *K* came from her grandmother's name Kathleen.

Recently an acclaimed female author from Spain, *Carmen Mola*, was revealed to be three men. Egad!

Lauded Spanish female crime writer revealed to be three men

By Hannah Ryan, CNN

🕐 Updated 4:21 AM ET, Mon October 18, 2021

Writers will also use pen names if they've written books outside their genre. Let's say a writer has written a spicy romance series about cowboys but wants to start writing cozy mysteries. It would probably be best to use a different pen name to separate the two genres. Nora Roberts is known for her romance books but publishes under the wildly popular J.D. Robb pseudonym for her science fiction books. I use T. Lockhaven for my adult books and Thomas Lockhaven for my children's books.

Some authors simply want to choose a pen name that is a better fit for their genre. If your last name is Lieberwitzaskinelle, and you want to write mystery books, you may want to go with something easy to remember and more fitting for your genre. Many writers choose names that imply action: Agatha Chase, Ethan Storm, Elizabeth Fox. You get the picture.

What if I've been writing for a long time and I have a huge following under my name?

That is certainly a reason not to change your name, especially if it is for a specific genre. Changing your name, if you have a substantial catalog of books and a huge following, could have negative repercussions. However, if you decide to begin writing in another genre, then depending on the chasm between the two genres, you may want to consider another pen name.

Do your research.

Once you choose a pen name, search on Amazon to see if there are other authors with that pen name. A friend of mine unfortunately didn't do this and found out much to her chagrin that there is another author that writes erotica under the same pen name. Now her children's books are mixed in with a myriad of erotica books. Make sure you check!

Once you have a unique pen name that you like, you may want to get a domain name that matches it. An inexpensive site for buying custom domain names is Namecheap.com. Let's say I want to register the name Agatha Chase, simply go to Namecheap.com, type the name you would like to register, and perform a search.

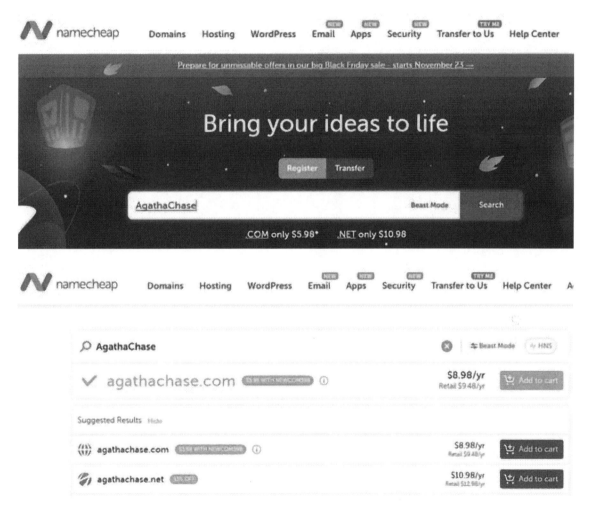

AgathaChase.com is available for less than $9.00. Now you can have a website created with your pen name!

Chapter 9
Sales Pitch

WRITING YOUR BLURB

To be honest, I should have said, writing your last will and testament with a sledgehammer and stone tablet. Blurb writing is one of the most painful, heart-wrenching, excruciating experiences you will go through as an author. I know. I know. You're shaking your head, "Don't sugarcoat it." Believe me, I wish I could. Hopefully—emphasis on the hope—I have culled together a formula that will help make this process a little easier for you, and in the end, you will craft a beautiful blurb that you will be proud of and send your prospective readers into a buying frenzy.

Let's start with the word blurb. May I ask *why they chose the word blurb*? I imagine blurb being the sound a bubble would make, breaking the water's surface as a person's last, dying breath. *Blurb. Blurb.* I must warn you, dear reader, proceed with caution.

WHAT IS A BLURB?

Raises eyebrows and shakes head. A blurb is a short description used to promote your book. Usually about 150–200 words. You're probably thinking to yourself, *easy*. I get to describe my seventy-thousand-word tome in two-hundred words. Nothing to it.

> "Oh, just wait," he smiles knowingly. "Dexter, be a good lad and cue up the evil grin and maniacal laughter. Lucile thinks it's easy to write a blurb."

We've all seen and read blurbs. If you go to a brick-and-mortar store, pick up a book and flip it over, the blurb is the paragraph or two that you see on the back cover. On Amazon's website or B&N's website, it's the description of the book, usually broken up into two or more paragraphs with a bolded title, containing important keywords relating to your genre.

Aside from your cover, this is most likely the most valuable piece of online real estate they will see. Your cover should capture their attention and your blurb should compel them to purchase your book.

WHAT A BLURB ISN'T

A blurb is *not* a synopsis of everything that happens in your book. A blurb should start with a bang and compel readers to buy. It should *not* reveal key elements of your book, especially if it's a whodunit. There should be zero spoilers in your blurb.

WHAT SHOULD I PUT IN MY BLURB?

Great question. Begin by introducing the protagonist and then asking yourself a few questions.

❋ Will the reader find the character relatable?

❋ Is it someone they want to spend time with?

❋ How do they fit into the story?

❋ What is the primary conflict they'll be facing in the story?

You need to show the reader that this book is for them. You can also compare your book to other successful, well-known books in your genre, but make sure you share what makes your book unique.

One way to get an idea of a successful blurb is to study ten to fifteen books in your genre that are performing well on Amazon.

❋ How do they introduce their protagonist?

❋ How do they hook you?

❋ What is the conflict?

❋ What problems are they facing?

❋ What's at stake if they're not successful?

❆ Do you notice any keywords in the title and the blurb that are unique to your genre? Amazon uses those keywords in its algorithm when it displays the readers' search results.

Let's practice writing a blurb together using the sample story, *Who Killed Mary Christmas*.

1 – Write the Hook

It's important to know that Amazon only displays the first few lines of your description. If you had a couple sentences to get people to read your book, what would you say?

If you're stuck, a great resource would be comments or reviews from your ARC group, or beta readers. If you've sent out pre-release copies and received some great reviews—such as a Kirkus review—you can use that review, or a snippet of the review, at the very beginning of your blurb. This gives readers even more proof that your book is worth their time—it uses social validation to let readers know that it's going to be wildly popular.

EXAMPLE 1 *Who killed Mary Christmas? A skillfully written cozy! Sure to be a bestseller this holiday season...* – Boston Globe

Interesting fact: There are currently over 1,500 people in the United States with the surname Christmas.

EXAMPLE 2 *T. Lockhaven channels Mary Higgins Clark in this marvelously-crafted whodunit* – New York Times

Here, the author is compared to an industry giant in the cozy publishing genre.

Amazon has included the heading styles for the description section of the book. I always configure my hook as a heading, so Amazon adds more weight to it when it comes to optimizing your Sales Page. To do this, go to your KDP bookshelf, select Kindle eBook Details.

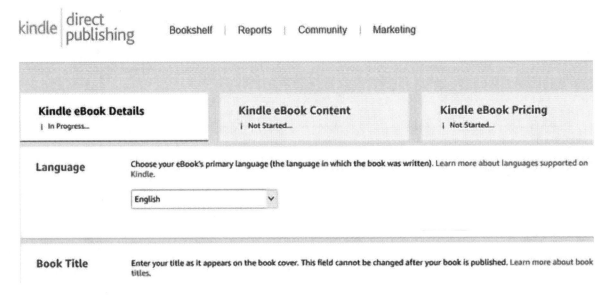

Scroll down to 'Description.' Highlight your hook, click on 'Format,' and select 'Heading 4.'

Add italics throughout your book as well to make your blurb look more appealing.

Here's how the book would look on Amazon.

2 – Who Is the Main Protagonist?

In the story *Who Killed Mary Christmas*, the protagonist is Michael Frost. Tell readers a little bit about who he is, and why they should care or even relate to him. In the book, Michael is a local coffee celebrity and has a large following. When he's not creating exotic new blends, he's working on his new poetry book and chumming around with his dog Bixby at the local parks. Think about who your readers will be. Who would they like to spend time with? Who will they care about? Go ahead and describe Michael in your own words. You can find this exercise at: christmascozymystery.com/resources.

_____

_____

_____

_____

_____

3 – Set the Stage for the Primary Conflict

It's Christmas Eve and Michael Frost has been accused of murder—a murder he didn't commit, or at least he thinks he didn't. He has no recollection from the night before. The police are steadily building up a substantial case against him. Describe the conflict in your own words without giving away too much!

_____

_____

_____

_____

_____

4 – Why Should Readers Care About Your Book?

What about your book is unique or different? What will compel them to purchase your book? The fact that you are writing for a very niche market is helpful. You're writing a Christmas cozy, so think of all the exciting elements that you can add into your blurb to motivate your reader to buy your book. Remember the reader reviews from the beginning of the book? What were some of the _must-haves_ the Christmas cozy mystery readers wrote about? Describe in your own words why people would want to read _Who Killed Mary Christmas_.

_____

_____

_____

_____

_____

5 – What's at Stake?

What happens if Michael fails? What is *truly* at stake here? If Michael doesn't find the killer, he'll most likely go to jail. He has to prove his innocence, or he'll lose his freedom. Smaller conflicts surround him too. He can't go back to his house. He can't work. He only has the clothes on his back, and the little bit of cash in his wallet. He can't use his credit cards or his phone. What can he do? Who can he trust? Describe in your own words what's at stake for Michael.

_____

_____

_____

_____

_____

_____

_____

_____

_____

6 – Call to Action

End the blurb with a bigger font, and easy-to-read Call to Action.

EXAMPLE Buy *Who Killed Mary Christmas* today to help Michael solve the mystery before time is up.

7 – Keywords

Now, let's go back and review your notes and make sure that you've included keywords that are specific to your genre. What are keywords that you would use for a Christmas Cozy or a Christmas Murder Mystery? I'll give you a hint, a lot of them are bolded in the reviews!

_____

_____

_____

_____

_____

_____

_____

Once you've got a list of keywords, you'll want to incorporate a few into your blurb copy. The important thing is not to overstuff your blurb with keywords. When authors do this, it's obvious to shoppers, and it's a turnoff.

You can download and print the blurb worksheet at the website: christmascozymystery.com/resources.

MAIN COMPONENTS OF A BLURB

In conclusion, your blurb should contain the following:

- ❀ Name of the book
- ❀ A catchy title and hook
- ❀ Keywords
- ❀ Reader reviews
- ❀ Comparison of your book to other books in your genre. How is yours unique?
- ❀ Introduction to the main character: Why should we care about them? How can readers align with them?
- ❀ Primary conflict: Don't give away key components of the book
- ❀ What's at stake? Why should we worry about the outcome of the protagonist? End this section with a cliffhanger.
- ❀ Call to Action

Chapter 10
Launching Your Book

PRE-ORDER

Pre-orders enable you to get visibility and sales for your book before it's released. Here's a few things that I do to let the world know that I've got a new release on the way.

AMAZON

The first thing I do is pray that people will love the book as much as I do. Then, I log into my KDP account to submit my book for Pre-Order. Simultaneously, I work with my editing team to make sure everything is perfect.

NOTE If your editors find mistakes and there are necessary rewrites that need to be made, don't worry. You can upload your changes to Amazon as needed. However, I would strongly suggest that you make sure all revisions and corrections are uploaded 72 hours before the release date.

Let me take you through the process step-by-step to submit your Pre-Order on Amazon. When you login to your KDP account, under 'Create a New Title,' click on 'Kindle eBook.'

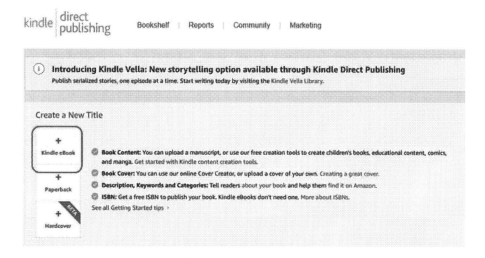

KINDLE EBOOK DETAILS

After clicking on 'Kindle eBook,' you will be taken to the following screen.

Kindle eBook Details	Kindle eBook Content	Kindle eBook Pricing
¦ In Progress...	¦ Not Started...	¦ Not Started...

Language   Choose your eBook's primary language (the language in which the book was written). Learn more about languages supported on Kindle.

> English ⌄

Book Title   Enter your title as it appears on the book cover. This field cannot be changed after your book is published. Learn more about book titles.

Book Title

> [   ]

Subtitle (Optional)

> [   ]

Series   If your book is part of a series, add series details so readers can easily find the titles on a single detail page. (Optional) Learn more

Add your title to an existing series or create a new one. Linked formats for this title will be automatically added to the series once setup is complete.

> Add series details

All things are not equal with Amazon. When you work with the e-book version of your book, you are able to make multiple changes to the *title*, *subtitle* and *author name*. However, for paperbacks and hardcover books, you cannot change the title, subtitle or author's name once it has been published. Furthermore, whatever you enter as the title and subtitle of your hardcopy book, it must match the cover.

For the e-book version, you can add keywords to your title and subtitle, even if the text isn't on the book cover. For example, on *Potion Commotion*, the book cover contains the following text:

❀ Merry and Moody Witch Cozy Mysteries
❀ Potion Commotion
❀ T. Lockhaven with S. T. White

However, I have entered the following text in my e-book:

❀ Title: Merry and Moody Witch Cozy Mysteries
❀ Subtitle: Potion Commotion: A Fast-Paced Paranormal Mystery Adventure Series of Female Protagonists with Animal Familiars for Teens and Adults

If you are writing a series, another identifier you'll want to add is which book it is in the series. If it's book three, make sure that you include that information somewhere on the book. It doesn't necessarily *have* to be on the front cover (even though that is visually helpful), it can be included in the blurb. If you don't include the series identifier, Amazon will ask you to update this information before they will link your books together.

What do I mean by linking the books together? If you are writing a series, you want Amazon to connect all of the books in the series together. So, if someone performs a search on one of your books, all of the books related in that series will show up. The following image was taken from a book's product details:

Books In This Series (9 Books)

Complete Series

Ava & Carol Detective Agency
Kindle Edition

 ‹

1

Ava & Carol Detective Agency: The Mystery of the Pharaoh's Diamonds: A Fun Middle Grade Mystery Adventure Action for Girls Ages 8-15 Children
› Thomas Lockhaven
★★★★☆ (37)
Kindle Edition
$2.99

2

Ava & Carol Detective Agency: The Mystery of Solomon's Ring
› Thomas Lockhaven
★★★★☆ (19)
Kindle Edition
$3.99

3

Ava & Carol Detective Agency: The Haunted Mansion (A Christmas Mystery Story)
› Thomas Lockhaven
★★★★☆ (20)
Kindle Edition
$3.99

4

Ava & Carol Detective Agency: Dognapped
› Thomas Lockhaven
★★★☆☆ (3)
Kindle Edition
$3.99

›

Scrolling down the page, you'll see the following fields.

Edition Number

You can provide an edition number if this title is a new edition of an existing book. What counts as a new edition? ∨

Edition Number (Optional)

Author

Enter the primary author or contributor. Pen names are allowed. Additional authors can be added in the Contributors field. Learn more about authorship.

Primary Author or Contributor

First name | Last name

Contributors

If others contributed to your book, you can add them and they'll be listed on the Amazon product detail page. For multiple authors, they'll appear in the same sequence as you add them below.

Contributors (Optional)

Author ∨ | First name | Last name | Remove

Add Another

Description

Summarize your book. This will be your product description on Amazon, so customers can learn more about your book. How do I format the description? ∨

B *I* U | ≔ ≔ | Format ∨ | Source

Since I'm publishing the book for the first time, I won't need to use the 'Edition Number' section. Next, I add in my pen name in the Author section. I also like to include and give credit to any contributors that helped with the book. Make sure you choose the correct type of contributor. I've made mistakes where I added my editor as an author. Luckily, I was able to update this information.

For the 'Description,' I paste in my blurb and format it to make it pop. From there, scroll down and you'll see 'Publishing Rights.'

Publishing Rights

○ I own the copyright and I hold the necessary publishing rights. What are publishing rights? ⌄

○ This is a public domain work. What is a public domain work? ⌄

Here, I select 'I own the copyright and I hold the necessary publishing rights.'

Next, you'll find the 'Keywords' and 'Categories' sections.

Keywords

Enter up to 7 search keywords that describe your book. How do I choose keywords? ⌄

Your Keywords (Optional)

Categories

Choose up to two browse categories. Why are categories important? ⌄

Set Categories

Amazon is a very powerful search engine. They want their customers to find what they're looking for. So, to help readers find the correct book, Amazon allows us to add up to seven keywords for free and place our book in two categories. I'll go over these in detail in the Advertising chapter.

Finally, you'll see 'Age and Grade Range' and the 'Pre-order' sections.

Since this is a Christmas murder mystery, I skip the 'Age and Grade Range' section.

As for 'Pre-order,' I select 'Make my Kindle eBook available for Pre-order.' Selecting the Pre-order option enables me to 'Set Release Date.'

I like to time my releases to hit over the weekends because more people are likely to see it. Another important reason to use Amazon Pre-Orders is because they send out notifications to anyone that is following you as an author. Make sure you ask people to follow you on Amazon!

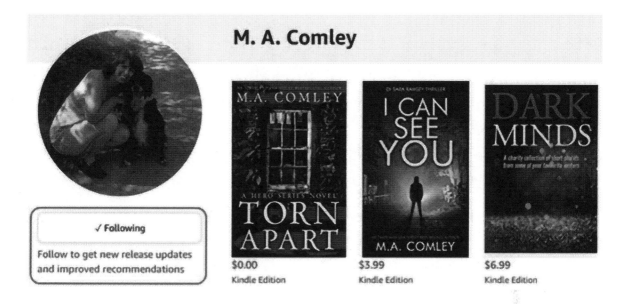

Amazon is unforgiving when it comes to missing deadlines. If you set up a release date and you don't release on time, Amazon can ban you from doing Pre-Orders for an entire year. This means that readers that follow you may not receive a notification from Amazon that you just released a new book.

If you're a little unorganized or not amazing at meeting deadlines, Amazon provides you with a safety net. (See, dear reader, Amazon can be reasonable, she just has high expectations.) Here's an option you might find helpful. You've finished 90% of your book, and you want your readers to know that it will be available soon. Amazon enables you to set your book up on Pre-Order as much as a year before the release date. This gives you some breathing room in case something happens, and it takes longer than expected to finish your book. Then, when you do finish, you can push the release date forward. Amazon doesn't punish you for publishing early. They do punish you if you miss your release date or cancel your Pre-Order.

So, think of Amazon as if you are going out on a date. She expects you to be ready, and on time. If she's waiting for you at the restaurant and you're not there on time, then you won't get another chance for a year. Plus, she may even remove you from her Facebook page, and that my friend, is simply tragic.

Once you've selected your Release Date, hit 'Save and Continue,' to head on over to 'Content.'

KINDLE EBOOK CONTENT

The 'Content' tab starts out with the following section.

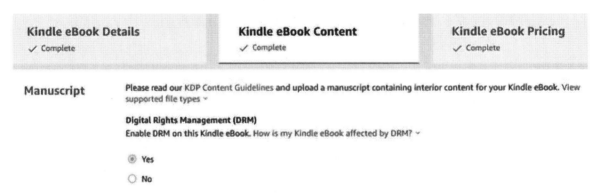

I always choose 'Yes' to Digital Rights Management. It is supposed to inhibit unauthorized distribution of the Kindle file of the book. If you select 'No,' readers would be able to share your book, which may lead to less sales.

IMPORTANT After you publish your book, you won't be able to change the DRM setting.

Next, I upload the eBook manuscript (even if it's still a work-in-progress) and the eBook cover. For this section, I always choose to upload an ePub file. The reason for this is because I want to make sure that any formatting I added to the book stays the same. I've put together a pre-formatted template which you can find on the website: christmascozymystery.com/resources.

You'll find it under 'Formatted Word Templates.' In the e-book file, I explain how I use the Calibre program to convert my file to an ePub.

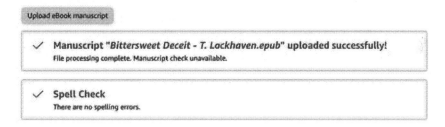

Next, I upload the eBook cover, then hit 'Launch Previewer' to make sure everything looks okay.

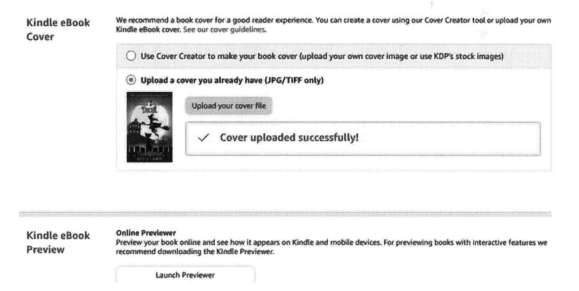

Finally, toward the bottom, you'll see the ISBN and Publisher fields.

Kindle eBook
ISBN

ISBN (Optional)
Kindle eBooks are not required to have an ISBN. What is an ISBN? ˅

Publisher (Optional)

Where do I get my ISBN (International Standard Book Number)? I buy my ISBNs in bulk from Bowker at myidentifiers.com.

Why don't I use an Amazon ISBN? Because I don't want my books to be limited to Amazon. If a bookstore decides to buy your book, then they are basically having to purchase from a competitor. They're likely to forgo the purchase.

Bowker has a VIP mailing list, which I encourage you to join. They do offer discounts every so often, so keep an eye out for them. I usually buy ISBN's in bulk whenever they run a special. For barcodes, I use a couple websites that generate them for free. You can find the links at: christmascozymystery.com/resources.

As for the 'Publisher' field, I type in my own publishing company. It defaults to 'Independently published' if left blank.

Now, you can hit 'Save and Continue' to move on to Pricing.

< Back to Details	Save as Draft	Save and Continue
		Next step: Pricing

KINDLE EBOOK PRICING

The following screen shows up in the Pricing tab.

KDP Select Enrollment

Maximize My Royalties with KDP Select (Optional)
With KDP Select, you can reach more readers, earn more money, and maximize your sales potential. Learn more about KDP Select. How Do I Enroll? ˅

Visit the Promotions Page to manage your KDP Select Enrollment

Territories

Select the territories for which you hold distribution rights. To enter the Kindle Storyteller contest, you need make your book available at least in Amazon.co.uk. Learn more about distribution rights.

◉ **All territories (worldwide rights)** What are worldwide rights? ˅

○ **Individual territories** What are Individual Territory rights? ˅

Primary marketplace

Choose the location where you expect the majority of your book sales.

| Amazon.com | ˅ |

Pricing, royalty, and distribution

Select a royalty plan and set your Kindle eBook list prices below
○ 35%   ◉ 70%

⎮ Your book file size after conversion is 2.02 MB.

Marketplace ˅	List Price ˅		Delivery ˅	Rate ˅	Royalty ˅
Amazon.com	$	USD	—	—	
	Must be $2.99-$9.99 ˅ All marketplaces are based on this price				

Please hear me out on this section. I know a lot of you are going to roll your eyes, but I am going to show you why I use a particular technique and I'll prove my theory with… *math*. And there go the eyerolls.

For my Pre-Orders I tend to go for $2.99 or $3.99 as the initial price point. If I'm starting a new series, I'll start with $2.99 for the first book and the rest are priced out at $3.99. I know, I know dear reader! Let me explain!

I know for a fact that the majority of the people that read cozy mysteries are on Kindle Unlimited. Thusly, I publish my cozies on KDP Select. If you publish with KDP select you can run promotions like the *Kindle Countdown Deal* and the *Free Book Promotion*.

If you're priced at $2.99, then you can do a Countdown Deal where your book is discounted to $0.99, then $1.99.

Now you will begin to see my logic. Buckle up!

Some authors set up their first books up for free or $0.99. That's completely fine and up to you. The reason I choose to start the series at $2.99 is because I've calculated the lost income from the number of returns on my e-books versus the profit I bring in.

Here comes the math!

If your book is priced between $2.99 and $9.99, Amazon pays you 70% in royalties. Any other amount would be at 35% royalties.

Therefore, at $0.99 on Amazon at 35% royalty, I would bring in $0.35 a book, which means that I would need to sell almost six books to equal the $2.00 I would receive from a $2.99 book at 70% royalty.

NOTE *Some readers are unethical. A Kindle reader can purchase your book, read the entire book and then return it, no questions asked, for a full refund from Amazon. I've had people purchase and read through my entire series and return it. It's annoying, but it's just something that comes with the territory.*

The math continues!

If it takes me ten clicks to sell a book, and each click cost me two cents, that means I just spent $0.20 to sell an e-book at $0.35. If they return the e-book after they've finished reading it, I've lost money. In order to break even, I would need to sell two more e-books, to make up for that $0.20 loss:

❀ Advertising cost → $0.60
❀ Books sold → 3
❀ Books returned → 1
❀ Royalties → $0.70
❀ Profit → $0.10

If I change the price of the book to $2.99, and sold two books instead of three because of the pricing, it would look like this:

❀ Advertising cost → $0.60
❀ Books sold → 2
❀ Books returned → 1
❀ Royalties → $2.00
❀ Profit → $1.40

So, according to my fancy drugstore calculator machine, $1.40 is higher than $0.10. This is hypothetical of course, the cost per click is usually higher than two cents. But at least I know it's easier to make a profit with $2.99. The other thing I noticed is when I've priced my books at $0.99 or marked them as free, it's been harder to sell the next in the series, readthrough rates drop and I tend to get lower star ratings. The readers seem to be less invested and harder to satisfy with free or lower price points.

Please don't take my word as gospel. Try and see what works for you. But after selling tens of thousands of books, this formula returns the most profit for me. I encourage you to experiment, and I look forward to hearing what works best for you!

GOODREADS

Why should I care about Goodreads? *Firstly*, it's owned by Amazon. *Secondly*, it has over 90 million registered users. *Thirdly*, this site is filled with ravenous readers. *Fourthly*, I actually don't have a fourthly. Actually, wait! Nope, I've got nothing.

I put my new books up on Goodreads as soon as I have descriptors or visual elements. This can be anything such as a title, a blurb or a book cover. Don't worry if you don't have a cover yet. I know a lot of authors who leave Goodreads's default placeholder cover, with a title that may or may not change in the future.

Why set this up? Several reasons. Let's say that you have followers that are reading your series and they're waiting for the next book. If you upload a work-in-progress to Goodreads, it lets them know that you are actively working on the next book. Readers like to know that their favorite series is being actively worked on.

I've had Goodreads readers mark my books to read and put them on their virtual shelves before I've even launched them. Another great thing about being proactive with Goodreads is they actively notify people through email and their newsfeed as soon as your book is launched.

NOTE If you've never released a book, you won't be able to claim an author page on Goodreads until your first book is Live on Amazon. You'll need to add your book to their system first. It can take up to seventy-two hours for them to approve it.

If the book hasn't been submitted through Amazon for a Pre-Order, you can go ahead and manually add in your book. If you have submitted a Pre-Order through Amazon, you'll first need to search for your book using the Goodreads search bar and see if it has been added to their database. If it hasn't, then hit 'Manually add a book,' on the right-hand side.

You'll be taken to the 'Add a New Book' section:

Go ahead and start by adding the 'Title' and the 'Author.' *This can always be updated when you claim your Author Profile through Goodreads. Otherwise, you won't be able to edit this section after you submit it.*

If you have an ASIN 'Amazon Standard Identification Number'—which you receive once your book has been submitted and is live on Amazon—then you can add this to your Goodreads listing. You can find the ASIN on your KDP Bookshelf.

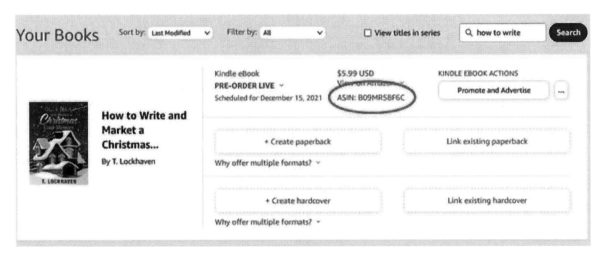

To add your ASIN to Goodreads, click the 'Click for ASIN' link. This will change the fields to allow you to enter the ASIN number instead of the ISBN.

If you add the ASIN instead of the ISBN, when a person clicks on the link for your book on Goodreads, they'll be taken straight to your Amazon Sales Page. If you add the ISBN number and the person clicks on the link for your book, it will redirect them to Amazon with your

ISBN number in their search bar. So, your best bet is to use the ASIN, so they go directly to your sales page.

→ The Most Important Section Is Work Settings ←

The most important part of the form is the publication date. If the "original publication date" is left blank, anyone who marked your book to read will not receive a notification when your book is released. Make sure this section is populated with the correct date.

Work Settings
Original publication date, characters, awards, and setting apply to all books in this work.

original title	
original publication date	year [ ] month [∨] day [∨]
media type	book [∨]

NOTE When you run a Goodreads Giveaway, your book is automatically added to the bookshelf of any Goodreads user who has entered the giveaway. So, if you are giving away 100 e-books, then your book will automatically show up in everyone's bookshelf who has entered the contest as 'marked-to-read.' If you don't have the 'original publication date' field filled out, you'll miss out on the free marketing email Goodreads sends out to these readers as soon as your book is released.

Setting the date in Goodreads is very similar to the way it's done in Amazon's Pre-Order section. However, Goodreads offers some benefits that Amazon doesn't. For instance, Goodreads allows you to set up your release date more than one year into the future. Yes, I wrote it that way to sound dramatic. And unlike Amazon, if you don't meet your publication date, Goodreads doesn't punish you. However, you may upset any readers who have marked your book to read.

I know what you are thinking. *All of this sounds easy, but what if I need help?* You're in luck, Goodreads has a team of helpers that they refer to as Librarians. They're there (not to be confused with *their there*, which means they have ownership of there, wherever there may be) to help you if you have questions or need assistance setting up your book correctly. To speak with a librarian, you'll need to join their group first. Here's the link: goodreads.com/group/show/220-goodreads-librarians-group

Once you've finished filling out the 'Add a new book' form, then you can submit it. Don't worry if you don't see the listing immediately. It can take a few minutes to show up in their system. Once the book is up, go to your book's page and click on the 'Want to Read' dropdown and select 'Currently Reading.'

Potion Commotion (Merry and Moody Witch Cozy Mysteries, #1)

by T. Lockhaven (Goodreads Author), S.T. White, Grace Lockhaven (Goodreads Author), Thomas Lockhaven (Goodreads Author)

★★★★ 4.50 · ⚑ Rating details · 50 ratings · 29 reviews

A charming paranormal cozy mystery filled with clever twists and turns.

Step into the world of Gwynevere Merry and Evelyn Moody as they attempt to catch an elusive murderer that seems to be able to predict their every move. A frightfully fun read filled with friendship, deception, magic, and oh yes... murder.

Praise for Potion Commotion

"I loved this one! Solving a murder mys ...more

Want to Read ▾

Read
Currently Reading
Want to Read

Add shelf

Refresh the page, and a new section will show up:

MY ACTIVITY   Edit

Review of	Potion Commotion (Merry and Moody Witch Cozy Mysteries, #1)
Rating	★★★★★
Shelves	currently-reading edit
Format	**Kindle Edition** edit
Status	● October 20, 2021 – Shelved
	● October 20, 2021 – Started Reading
Progress	I am ___ % done With Potion Commotion
Review	Write a review
	comment

Notice the little box after 'Progress' tag, where it says, "I am ___ % done." Click on the box, and the following will show up.

Progress	I am ___ % done With Potion Commotion
	Add a quote, comment or note
	Save Progress

I use this section to keep my followers updated as to my work-in-progress when I'm writing a book. So, if I've written 5% of the book,

I type the number five into the percentage box, and in the text box below it, I give my readers a small update as to my progress. Here's an example:

I'm currently working on a new story about a man who winds up in a small town with a suitcase full of cash. He has no idea who he is or how he got there. The only thing he knows for certain is that he plays the piano phenomenally well, and he has a compulsion to cook. I'm having a blast creating a back story and pulling in tiny shards of memories from his past.

After I've typed this little blast of information, I hit "Save Progress" and any followers that I have will see my update on their Goodreads News Feed.

The next thing I would suggest that you do is hit the 'Write a review' button. Don't give yourself a star-rating, you are going to use the review section for something other than giving yourself a review. The Goodreads community frowns upon authors who give themselves five stars.

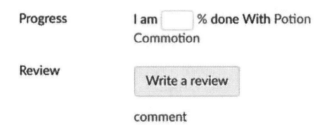

So why am I pressing the 'Write a review' button? You are going to leave a message for people about your book. For example:

I'm currently working on a new mystery! It's about a guy with amnesia who winds up…

Using this method, you can give readers a timeline as to when you expect the book to be released and you can give them a little info about the book. You can also let them know if they have any questions to post them, and that you'll get to them as quickly as possible.

As you're writing your book, keep updating the percentage done in Goodreads. This helps readers to visualize the progression and helps to build excitement.

The other neat thing about adding a book to 'currently-reading' is that if anyone goes to your profile page, they'll see your book. Goodreads shows three 'currently-reading' books on your profile, so you can use this as a marketing strategy, especially once you launch the book.

Chapter 11
Advertising

SOCIAL PROOF

Before I begin advertising my book, I work on getting at least ten reviews ready for my book launch.

First, make sure you give yourself enough time to get the reviews you need. I usually give my ARC readers two weeks to read and leave reviews. I upload digital copies of my book to BookSprout.co and StoryOriginApp.com.

BookSprout recommends giving your readers 2-3 weeks. It does take time to build up followers on these sites, but they are definitely worth it. Readers will download a free copy of your book, read it and review it. Again, be patient. It will take a bit of time to get a following. However, once you do, you'll have several reviews posted for you on your preferred stores like Amazon, Goodreads and Barnes & Noble.

If there isn't enough interest in your book to get the reviews you need using these platforms, there are Facebook groups and Goodreads Groups that will read and review the book for you.

Once you have a good number of reviews, it becomes much easier to advertise your book. When I was first getting started writing books and publishing them, I was crushed with one-star reviews. I listened to an editor that gave me bad advice, and in return I got a plethora of one-star reviews. My sales plummeted. I hired a new editor, rewrote the book, got beta readers behind it and relaunched. It cost me a fortune to get readers interested in my book because of the previous low-star ratings.

However, after a few weeks and spending a fortune on advertising, readers began giving it a second chance. Those one- and two-star reviews were replaced with four- and five-star reviews. Then I saw something amazing happen. The more reviews that came in, the more my books sold. It took some time, but the reviews did their job. They were a form of social validation, that the book was worth reading.

Don't worry if they're not all 5-star reviews. A variety of 3- to 5-star reviews makes it more believable for prospective buyers. There are also some reviewers that refuse to give 5-star reviews to any book. Some of my beta readers only give 4-star reviews. Write the best book you can, edit the heck out of it, and release it into the wild, knowing you did the best you could do.

Also, remember, you will never be able to please everyone. No matter what you do, your writing style won't appeal to everyone. People can be harsh. I've received one-star reviews with comments like:

❧ *Not to my liking*

❧ *Author used the word devil and frightened my child* (Interestingly enough, the book was titled *The Curse of the Red Devil*)

❧ *Book arrived two days late*

A fellow author friend of mine posted to Facebook a couple days ago that he received a one-star review. The person wrote, "Not Bought" as the title of the review and "Never bought it" as the comment.

Again, do the best you can, and realize there will always be people that aren't satisfied. Mick Jagger being one of those people. I heard from a very reputable source that he said, "I Can't Get No Satisfaction."

AMAZON – FREE ADVERTISING

Amazon keyword marketing—Free and easy to implement. Hooray!

KEYWORDS

One way to have a higher ranking on Amazon is to have keywords in the *title* or *subtitle* of your book. For example, if you wrote a *paranormal cozy mystery*, you would definitely benefit by having that keyword phrase on the cover of your book. If it's not, make sure you add it in the kindle version's *title* or *subtitle*.

Remember, for hardcopies, Amazon prevents you from adding anything other than what's on the front cover of your book. If you're unable to add "paranormal cozy mystery" in the *title* or *subtitle*, then add it in one of the 7 keyword boxes. You can find this by going to your Amazon KDP Bookshelf and clicking on the 'Edit eBook details' link.

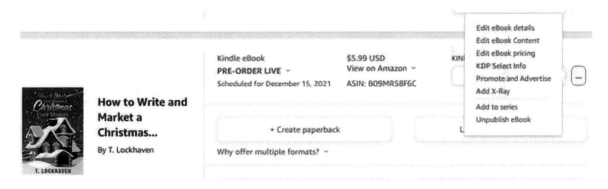

Scroll down to find the 'Keywords' section.

Keywords Enter up to 7 search keywords that describe your book. How do I choose keywords? ˅

Your Keywords (Optional)

Publisher Rocket

If you're looking for keyword ideas, the best investment you can make is to purchase Publisher Rocket. The link to the product is on the website christmascozymystery.com/resources.

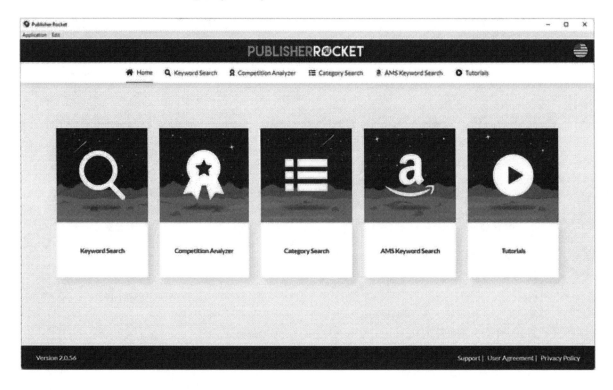

When I purchased it a couple years ago, I paid $97, and it has paid for itself over and over again. I literally use Publisher Rocket daily. Dave

Chesson, the creator, offers phenomenal support and is constantly adding new features. I've found him to be exceptionally responsive to questions and he quickly releases tutorials and videos explaining the new software features. I can't recommend his product enough.

Here are some examples showing Publisher Rocket in action. I searched on the keyword string 'Christmas cozy mysteries' and 'Christmas murder mysteries' and ran reports displaying the results from October, November and December. I did this so you can see the difference of the average searches per month from Amazon customers and the average monthly earnings of those specific keywords.

EB means I searched the keyword in e-books. **B** means I searched for the keyword for books.

OCTOBER: EB – CHRISTMAS COZY MYSTERIES

Keyword	Average Pages	Number Of Competitors	Average Price	Average Monthly Earnings	Est. Amazon Searches/Month	Competitive Score	
christmas cozy mysteries	247	3,454	$7	$1,582	1,506	40	≔
christmas cozy mysteries 2021	459	227	$5	$3,519	2,110	41	≔
christmas cozy mysteries kindle	266	3,435	$6	$1,009	1,471	65	≔
christmas cozy mysteries paperback	465	280	$6	$2,718	331	25	≔

NOVEMBER: EB – CHRISTMAS COZY MYSTERIES

Keyword	Average Pages	Number Of Competitors	Average Price	Average Monthly Earnings	Est. Amazon Searches/Month	Competitive Score	
christmas cozy mysteries	354	3,612	$5	$4,237	1,694	85	
christmas cozy mysteries 2021	422	350	$6	$3,294	2,119	65	
christmas cozy mysteries 2021 kindle unlimited	384	101	$4	$1,175	252	57	
christmas cozy mysteries free	155	167	$0	$0	13,321	65	
christmas cozy mysteries kindle	382	3,598	$4	$1,152	1,371	20	
christmas cozy mysteries kindle unlimited	404	234	$4	$2,110	280	65	
christmas cozy mysteries joanne fluke	419	46	$7	$1,375	<100	21	
christmas cozy mysteries paperback	384	317	$3	$1,498	331	65	
christmas cozy mysteries free kindle books	118	168	$0	$0	1,136	65	
christmas cozy mysteries kindle books	397	3,605	$4	$3,730	479	85	
christmas cozy mysteries kindle unlimitedbooks 2021	221	3	$0	$0	<100	65	
free christmas cozy mysteries	112	170	$0	$0	9,003	65	

DECEMBER: EB – CHRISTMAS COZY MYSTERIES

Keyword	Average Pages	Number Of Competitors	Average Price	Average Monthly Earnings	Est. Amazon Searches/Month	Competitive Score	
christmas cozy mysteries	389	3,749	$6	$14,284	1,586	85	
christmas cozy mysteries 2021	272	508	$6	$34,645	2,224	65	
christmas cozy mysteries 2021 kindle unlimited	523	153	$4	$3,869	290	65	
christmas cozy mysteries boxed set	1,230	182	$4	$1,026	<100	25	
christmas cozy mysteries free	115	221	$0	$0	13,232	65	
christmas cozy mysteries free kindle books	132	221	$0	$0	1,262	65	
christmas cozy mysteries kindle	248	3,814	$5	$7,427	1,381	80	
christmas cozy mysteries kindle unlimited	397	292	$3	$36,476	286	60	
christmas cozy mysteries joanne fluke	460	58	$7	$3,432	<100	44	
christmas cozy mysteries paperback	400	402	$4	$1,255	331	32	
free christmas cozy mysteries							

OCTOBER: B – CHRISTMAS COZY MYSTERIES

Keyword	Average Pages	Number Of Competitors	Average Price	Average Monthly Earnings	Est. Amazon Searches/Month	Competitive Score	
christmas cozy mysteries	249	>1,200	$14	$633	571	33	
christmas cozy mysteries paperback	275	>1,200	$10	$571	259	20	

More Info

NOVEMBER: B – CHRISTMAS COZY MYSTERIES

Keyword	Average Pages	Number Of Competitors	Average Price	Average Monthly Earnings	Est. Amazon Searches/Month	Competitive Score	
christmas cozy mysteries	274	>1,200	$13	$2,188	571	61	
christmas cozy mysteries 2021	258	485	$11	$2,487	1,532	25	
christmas cozy mysteries paperback	253	>1,200	$9	$614	252	28	
christmas cozy mysteries free kindle books	97	>1,200	$1	$0	638	85	
christmas cozy mysteries joanne fluke	456	57	$14	$1,272	<100	13	
christmas cozy mysteries kindle books	219	>1,200	$2	$477	315	73	
christmas cozy mysteries kindle unlimitedbooks 2021	221	3	$0	$0	<100	65	
free christmas cozy mysteries	135	>1,200	$2	$248	2,795	85	

More Info

DECEMBER: B – CHRISTMAS COZY MYSTERIES

Keyword	Average Pages	Number Of Competitors	Average Price	Average Monthly Earnings	Est. Amazon Searches/Month	Competitive Score	
christmas cozy mysteries	278	>1,200	$14	$916	597	49	
christmas cozy mysteries 2021	257	681	$9	$11,177	1,457	25	
christmas cozy mysteries paperback	341	>1,200	$14	$2,106	250	53	
christmas cozy mysteries books	340	>1,200	$13	$2,115	1,184	77	
christmas cozy mysteries free kindle books	155	>1,200	$1	$87	613	77	
christmas cozy mysteries joanne fluke	476	70	$12	$1,128	<100	20	
christmas cozy mysteries kindle	394	>1,200	$6	$5,363	1,357	85	

More Info

OCTOBER: EB – CHRISTMAS MURDER MYSTERIES

Keyword	Average Pages ⇕	Number Of Competitors ⇕	Average Price ⇕	Average Monthly Earnings ⇕	Est. Amazon Searches/Month ⇕	Competitive Score ⇕
christmas murder mysteries	306	2,875	$8	$1,307	870	33

More Info

NOVEMBER: EB – CHRISTMAS MURDER MYSTERIES

Keyword	Average Pages ⇕	Number Of Competitors ⇕	Average Price ⇕	Average Monthly Earnings ⇕	Est. Amazon Searches/Month ⇕	Competitive Score ⇕
christmas murder mysteries	335	3,019	$7	$3,408	870	44
christmas murder mysteries books	274	3,008	$7	$2,373	287	45

More Info

DECEMBER: EB – CHRISTMAS MURDER MYSTERIES

Keyword	Average Pages ⇕	Number Of Competitors ⇕	Average Price ⇕	Average Monthly Earnings ⇕	Est. Amazon Searches/Month ⇕	Competitive Score ⇕
christmas murder mysteries	325	3,145	$7	$8,718	1,377	85
christmas murder mysteries books	318	3,136	$6	$5,991	330	85

More Info

OCTOBER: B – CHRISTMAS MURDER MYSTERIES

Keyword	Average Pages ⇕	Number Of Competitors ⇕	Average Price ⇕	Average Monthly Earnings ⇕	Est. Amazon Searches/Month ⇕	Competitive Score ⇕
christmas murder mysteries	313	>1,200	$13	$2,305	<100	28

More Info

NOVEMBER: B – CHRISTMAS MURDER MYSTERIES

Keyword	Average Pages ⇕	Number Of Competitors ⇕	Average Price ⇕	Average Monthly Earnings ⇕	Est. Amazon Searches/Month ⇕	Competitive Score ⇕
christmas murder mysteries	342	>1,200	$12	$1,351	<100	73
christmas murder mysteries books	336	>1,200	$10	$1,900	691	80

More Info

DECEMBER: B – CHRISTMAS MURDER MYSTERIES

Keyword	Average Pages	Number Of Competitors	Average Price	Average Monthly Earnings	Est. Amazon Searches/Month	Competitive Score	
christmas murder mysteries	313	>1,200	$12	$1,653	<100	55	
christmas murder mysteries 2021	300	786	$10	$8,991	648	57	
christmas murder mysteries books	300	>1,200	$11	$1,403	686	69	

In case the screenshots are hard to read, I drew up a table below that shows the difference between each month. Just an FYI, I added all the rows from the images (except for >100) to give you an overall idea of searches and sales:

Keyword	Month	Average Monthly Searches	Average Monthly Earnings
E-Book Christmas Cozy Mysteries	October	5,418	$8,828
	November	29,786	$18,571
	December	20,592	$102,414
Book Christmas Cozy Mysteries	October	830	$1,204
	November	6,103	$7,286
	December	5,458	$22,892
E-Book Christmas Murder Mysteries	October	870	$1,307
	November	1137	$5,781
	December	1,707	$14,709
Book Christmas Murder Mysteries	October	>100	$2,305
	November	691	$3,251
	December	1,334	$12,047

Let's talk about keywords. As an author you can enter up to seven target keywords into the Kindle keyword boxes. Each box allows up to 50 characters. The question is what keywords should I use?

Keywords   Enter up to 7 search keywords that describe your book. How do I choose keywords? ⌄

Your Keywords (Optional)

Dave Chesson, the creator of Publisher Rocket, ran a massive experiment to see how to get the best keyword results. They chose 120 books (a mixture of fiction and non-fiction) from authors. Then, they asked each author for the keywords they used in the 7 boxes. Finally, they unleashed a special web crawler developed by their team. Over a period of several days, the crawler checked over 100,000 keyword possibilities.

The results, *Thomas Lockhaven is a genius!* Okay, not really. Don't act so surprised. There was still another experiment to be run.

Once they had the data from the previous experiment, they asked the authors to change their data. Some of the authors had filled in as many keywords as they could, using as many characters as they could in each field, while others had used a specific keyword phrase. Then the crawler was run once again. Here's what they found out.

1. Filling in all 50 characters in the Kindle keyword box does index your book for more keywords.
2. Amazon uses all variations of the words that you enter into the keyword box.

3. Targeting a specific phrase does help with rankings. Also, the more specific you are in your phrasing in the keyword box, the higher you'll rank for that search result. Remember though, your ranking will depend on the amount of competition you have for that keyword or keyword phrase.

4. It's better to put your keyword in the Title and Subtitle than the Keyword Box. Their research showed a 37% increase in rankings when the author had the keyword phrase in their title or subtitle. This shows that those two spots have a larger effect on ranking than the 7 keyword boxes.

Here's what Dave Chesson recommends to launch a successful keyword campaign in Amazon.

1. Find 1-3 keywords or keyword phrases that are extremely relevant to your book. Think about that perfect string of words that your target audience would type into Amazon to find your book. You can actually use Publisher Rocket to find out the exact keyword phrases people are searching on. Place those in the first three keyword boxes.

   Here's an example showing the search string for "Supernatural Cozy Mystery". The competition score is based on a scale from 1-100 as to 100 being how difficult it is to rank for that keyword phrase.

Keyword	Average Pages ≑	Number Of Competitors ≑	Average Price ≑	Average Monthly Earnings ≑	Est. Amazon Searches/Month ≑	Competitive Score ≑	
supernatural cozy mystery	280	11,674	$5	$13,116	1,023	53	≡
supernatural cozy mysteries	226	11,675	$5	$13,823	1,826	53	≡

2. Fill in the rest of the boxes with niche or genre specific terms and phrases. For example, if you have the following text strings in your keyword boxes, "Paranormal Cozy Mystery" and "Paranormal Murder Mystery Small Town Fantasy Witch," Amazon will rank you higher in the search results if a customer searches on "Paranormal Cozy Mystery", but it will also index you on several other searches like:

❀ Paranormal Cozy Mystery
  ➤ Mystery Cozy Paranormal
  ➤ Mystery Paranormal Cozy
  ➤ Paranormal Mystery Cozy
❀ Paranormal Murder Mystery Small Town Fantasy Witch
  ➤ Small Town Paranormal Mystery
  ➤ Witch Murder Mystery
  ➤ Fantasy Small Town Witch

And so on, the only downside is you'll rank lower since it's not an exact match.

Amazon Search

If you don't have Publisher Rocket, you can still find keywords by going to Amazon.com. On the left-hand side, where it says 'All', select Books or Kindle Store—depending on which version you're working with—then start typing in a keyword.

For example, paranormal cozy will bring you the following:

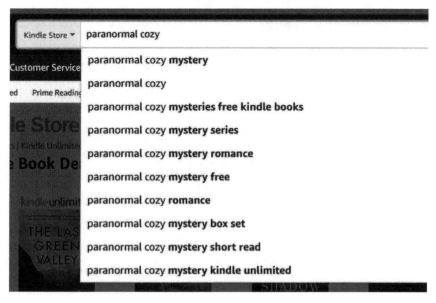

Continue doing this, starting with different keywords, to find your keyword phrases.

CATEGORIES

Amazon lets you choose two categories in the 'Edit eBook details' tab. There are several you can choose from, as long as your book contains an element of the category type you are choosing.

When you hit 'Set Categories,' you'll see the following image:

For cozies, you'll want to search in 'Fiction.' You can find 'Cozy' by selecting the 'Mystery & Detective' header.

Choose categories (up to two):

- Mystery & Detective
  - ☐ General
  - ☐ Collections & Anthologies
  - ☐ Cozy
  - ☐ Hard-Boiled
  - ☐ Historical
  - ☐ International Mystery & Crime
  - ☐ Police Procedural
  - ☐ Private Investigators
  - ☐ Traditional British
  - ☐ Women Sleuths

For your other category, I recommend trying to find another section within 'Fiction' so you can hit two different audiences.

Since it's a Christmas cozy, you can select your second category as 'Holidays.'

Choose categories (up to two):

- Fantasy
- ☐ Gay
- ☐ Ghost
- ☐ Gothic
- ☐ Hispanic & Latino
- ☐ Historical
- ☐ Holidays
- ☐ Horror
- ☐ Humorous
- ☐ Jewish
- ☐ Legal

Even though Amazon only lets you choose two categories, there is a little-known technique where you can rank in 10-12 categories.

Publisher Rocket

If you have Publisher Rocket, you can quickly search for the different categories you'd like to rank in. For example, I'll type in 'mystery' in the search bar, select eBook, and it'll show me all categories that contain the word 'mystery' in the Kindle Store.

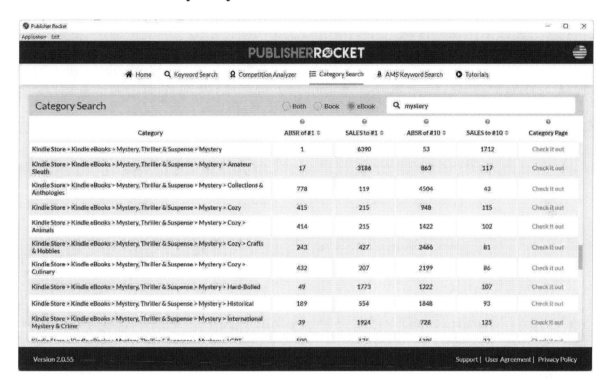

ABSR stands for Amazon's Best Sellers Rank. You can also find this information on a book's Sales Page, under Product details. In the following Product details example, you can see that the book ranks #1 in three different categories.

Product details

ASIN : B083J7QQ89

Publisher : Thomas & Mercer (November 1, 2020)

Publication date : November 1, 2020

Language : English

File size : 1991 KB

Text-to-Speech : Enabled

Screen Reader : Supported

Enhanced typesetting : Enabled

X-Ray : Enabled

Word Wise : Enabled

Print length : 332 pages

Lending : Not Enabled

Best Sellers Rank: #4 in Kindle Store (See Top 100 in Kindle Store)

   #1 in Serial Killer Thrillers

   #1 in Police Procedurals (Kindle Store)

   #1 in Murder Thrillers

Customer Reviews: ★★★★½ ⌄   30,547 ratings

According to Publisher Rocket, if we chose the category that ends in *Mystery, Thriller & Suspense > Mystery*, you would need to sell more than 6,390 e-books in one day to get to the number one spot in that category.

Category	ABSR of #1	SALES to #1	ABSR of #10	SALES to #10	Category Page
Kindle Store > Kindle eBooks > Mystery, Thriller & Suspense > Mystery	1	6390	53	1712	Check it out

That's *way* too much competition. So it's best to find the most specific categories. A good category to pick would be, *Thriller & Suspense > Mystery > Cozy > Culinary*.

Category	ABSR of #1	SALES to #1	ABSR of #10	SALES to #10	Category Page
Kindle Store > Kindle eBooks > Mystery, Thriller & Suspense > Mystery > Cozy > Culinary	432	207	2199	86	

It'll be much easier to get into the top 100 in that category, therefore helping with visibility and free marketing from Amazon. This is especially important when you're just releasing on Amazon as well because of the Amazon Hot New Releases section. Here's a screenshot of our book *The Christmas Thief* as number two in the Amazon Hot New Releases.

For one month, after your release, if you have enough sales, your book can show up in that section. You can find the 'Hot New Releases' section by clicking on a category. You can either click on the category through a book's product details, like in the below example.

Best Sellers Rank: #7,964 in Kindle Store (See Top 100 in Kindle Store)

   #63 in Witch & Wizard Mysteries

   #65 in Ghost Mysteries

   #75 in Magical Realism

Customer Reviews: ⭐⭐⭐⭐½ ⌄   3,293 ratings

Or you can find it by using the Amazon search bar, which I'll explain in a bit. In this case, I'll select the category 'Witch & Wizard Mysteries.' Amazon has been changing the look a bit through the years, so it may look different on your end. This is what it looks like now:

You'll see on the bottom left, it says 'New Releases in Witch & Wizard Mysteries.' When I click on that, it takes me to the following page:

This is where your book has a chance to show up for the first month after your release. I would check on the last book in this section, #100, and take a look at their Best Sellers Rank to see if it's something I can beat. Today, #100 has the following numbers:

Best Sellers Rank: #93,087 in Kindle Store (See Top 100 in Kindle Store)

 #796 in Psychic Mysteries

 #1,155 in Witch & Wizard Mysteries

 #1,234 in Ghost Mysteries

Customer Reviews: ★★★★☆ ∨ 3 ratings

Rank #93,087 is doable. That means that I would probably need to sell two to three e-books in a day to beat this book and rank #100 in the 'New Releases in Witch & Wizard Mysteries' section.

If you do end up hitting #1, Amazon rewards you with a #1 Hot New Release badge. Here's the same book *The Christmas Thief* that was in the 'Hot New Releases' section with the #1 New Release badge.

Ava & Carol Detective Agency: The Christmas Thief Kindle Edition
by Thomas Lockhaven (Author), Andrea VanRyken (Editor), David Aretha (Editor), Grace Lockhaven (Editor)   Format: Kindle Edition

★★★★★ ∨ 3 ratings

Book 9 of 9: Ava & Carol Detective Agency

#1 New Release in Children's Detectives Books

› See all formats and editions

Kindle	Paperback
$0.00 kindleunlimited	$12.99 ✓prime
Read with Kindle Unlimited to also enjoy access to over 1 million more titles $3.99 to buy	1 New from $12.99

Move over Santa! This year, Ava and Carol are figuring out who's naughty or nice.

A Christmas Special Edition

There's a time of year that's full of cheer—but this December, not everything is quite so merry for Ava and
‹ Read more

Amazon Search

Another way to find categories is, navigate to Amazon.com. On the left-hand side of the Search Bar where it says 'All,' click the drop-down button, and select either Books or Kindle Store. Then hit 'Enter' on your keyboard or click on the magnifying glass icon.

Let's say you selected Kindle Store.

On the left-hand side, under *Department*, you'll see the Kindle store and its categories.

Select *Kindle eBooks*, then *Mystery, Thriller & Suspense*.

‹ Kindle eBooks

Mystery, Thriller & Suspense

   Crime Fiction

   Mystery

   Science Fiction

   Suspense

   Thrillers

The Man Who Died Twice: A Thursday...
★★★★☆ 4,902
Kindle Price: $13.99

Dying Breath
★★★★☆ 151
Kindle Price: $3.99

Clues,
★★
Kindle

Click on *Mystery* and you'll see several categories you can choose from.

Department

‹ Kindle Store

‹ Kindle eBooks

‹ Mystery, Thriller & Suspense

Mystery

   Amateur Sleuth

   Black & African American

   Collections & Anthologies

   Cozy

   Hard-Boiled

   Historical

   International Mystery & Crime

The Dark Hours

Book 4 of 4: Renée Ballard

★★★★☆ ⌄ 12,097

Kindle Edition

$14⁹⁹ $29.00

Available instantly

In this example, I'll choose *Cozy*. For your book, make sure you pick a category that reflects your story.

Department

‹ Kindle Store

‹ Kindle eBooks

‹ Mystery, Thriller & Suspense

‹ Mystery

Cozy

   Animals

   Crafts & Hobbies

   Culinary

Moods & Themes

☐ Action-packed

☐ Dark

☐ Disturbing

☐ Fun

☐ Gory

The Thursday Murder Club: A Novel (A Thursday Murder Club Mystery Book 1)

Book 1 of 3: A Thursday Murder Club Mystery

★★★★☆ ⌄ 67,295

Kindle Edition

$11⁹⁹ $17.00

Available instantly

Let's say your book is a Christmas cozy and a lot of the story is about how the amateur sleuth's pet dog helps them sniff out crime, you may then choose *Animals* under the *Cozy* category.

Your search string would look like this:

> Kindle eBooks > Mystery, Thriller & Suspense > Mystery > Cozy > Animals

Now you have a niche market where your book will have a better chance of ranking higher in Amazon.

NOTE This is another reason I highly recommend Publisher Rocket. The software will save you a lot of time and work.

When searching for categories, the more niche the category, the better.

Here are a few examples you can choose from for cozies. Please keep in mind that Amazon is constantly changing their category listings.

➤ Kindle eBooks > Literature & Fiction > Action & Adventure > Mystery, Thriller & Suspense > Mystery

➤ Kindle eBooks > Literature & Fiction > Small Town & Rural

➤ Kindle eBooks > Literature & Fiction > Women's Fiction > Fantasy

➤ Kindle eBooks > Literature & Fiction > Women's Fiction > Mystery, Thriller & Suspense > Women Sleuths

➤ Kindle eBooks > Mystery, Thriller & Suspense > Mystery > Cozy

➤ Kindle eBooks > Mystery, Thriller & Suspense > Mystery > Cozy > Animals

➤ Kindle eBooks > Mystery, Thriller & Suspense > Mystery > Cozy > Crafts & Hobbies

➤ Kindle eBooks > Mystery, Thriller & Suspense > Mystery > Cozy > Culinary

- Kindle eBooks > Mystery, Thriller & Suspense > Mystery > Amateur Sleuth
- Kindle eBooks > Mystery, Thriller & Suspense > Mystery > Series
- Kindle eBooks > Mystery, Thriller & Suspense > Suspense > Paranormal
- Kindle eBooks > Mystery, Thriller & Suspense > Suspense > Paranormal > Psychics
- Kindle eBooks > Mystery, Thriller & Suspense > Suspense > Paranormal > Vampires
- Kindle eBooks > Mystery, Thriller & Suspense > Suspense > Paranormal > Werewolves & Shifters

ADDING YOUR CATEGORIES

Did you know that you can add a lot more than the three categories you may see on your Book's Sales Page? You can, but you'll have to contact Amazon directly to do so. Here's how! Once you've compiled your list of other categories, you'll need to work with Amazon to add the additional categories for you.

After I submit my book and it's 'Live' on Amazon, I buy a copy. Why? Because when a book is purchased, Amazon will rank you and then you can see the categories that you are ranked in.

Then, I refer back to the list of categories that I've made and cross off any that my book is already listed in. Once I have that information, I navigate to the KDP Bookshelf section, scroll to the bottom of the page and hit the *Contact Us* link.

 Facebook Twitter

From the options given, I select 'Amazon Store & Product Detail Page,' then select 'Update Amazon Categories.'

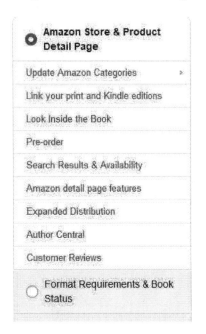

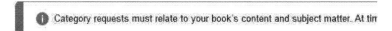

You'll have to send them your ASIN, and then the list of categories you would like to show up in. Remember, the ASIN is found in the KDP Bookshelf section.

AMAZON – PAID ADVERTISING

I use free advertising to promote organic sales as well as Amazon Marketing Services. In this section, I'll talk about setting up ads to promote your book.

SETTING UP YOUR CAMPAIGN

Navigate to your KDP Bookshelf and select 'Promote and Advertise'.

On the right-hand side, you'll see a button titled 'Run an Ad Campaign.' Choose the marketplace you want to start advertising in and hit 'Create an ad campaign.'

Run an Ad Campaign

With Amazon Ads, you set your budget, targeting, and timing. You pay only when shoppers click your ads. To create an ad campaign, choose the Amazon marketplace where you want the ad to appear. To advertise this book in multiple marketplaces, repeat this step for each marketplace. Learn more

Choose a marketplace:

Choose... ∨

Create an ad campaign

You must select a marketplace where you would like to advertise your book from the drop-down menu above.

Register for an Amazon Ads webinar

Enroll in free Amazon Ads training courses

This will take you to the following page:

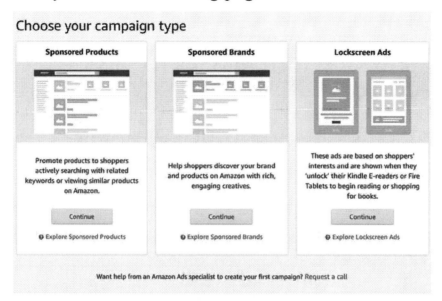

If you haven't already set up your billing information, you can find that on the left-hand side of the screen.

You'll see the Administration gear icon toward the bottom. Click on that, then on 'Billing and payments.'

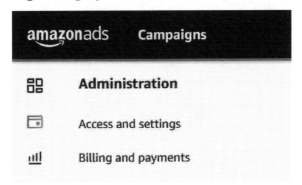

Once you've set up your financial information, you can create your ads. Hooray! Now, let's go back to creating campaigns by hitting the second icon on the left-hand side.

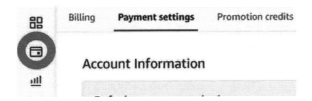

Once again, you'll be taken to the campaign type screen.

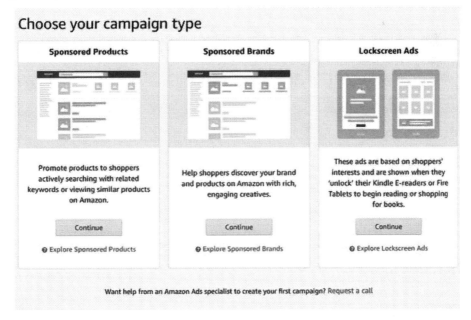

I always use Sponsored Products. They've been the least costly and have generated the most sales. Hit the 'Continue' button, to begin creating your campaign.

AUTO-TARGETING

Amazon describes Auto-Targeting as: "Amazon will target keywords and products that are similar to the product in your ad." In this next section, I'll go step-by-step to explain exactly what Amazon needs:

Settings

Campaign name ⓘ

    H2WXmasCozy Auto 12/05/2021

Portfolio ⓘ

    No Portfolio   ⌄

Start ⓘ   **End** ⓘ

    Dec 10, 2021   No end date

❧ **Campaign name** – I'll start with this first text box. When setting up your campaigns, don't give them generic names like, campaign one or campaign two. Name them so you can tell what the campaign is about. For example, let's say I'm advertising this How-To book and setting up an Auto Targeting campaign. I would name it: H2WXmasCozy Auto 12/05/2021. I have part of my book's title. I have Auto in the description to let me know it's an auto-targeted ad, and its launch date.

❦ **Portfolio** – I like to separate my ads by book, series, or genre. In this example, I'll create a 'Portfolio' named *NF* for *non-fiction* (you can always rename it). Portfolios make it a lot easier to analyze how each group of books is performing.

❦ **Start** – I tend to use today's date, but it depends on your goal. Maybe you only want to advertise during Christmastime. Amazon enables you to set up your ads for a specific date period.

❦ **End** – I tend to leave this at 'No end date,' but of course, you can decide what works best for you.

Daily budget ❶

$ [   ]

Targeting

◉ Automatic targeting
  Amazon will target keywords and products that are similar to the product in your ad.

○ Manual targeting
  Choose keywords or products to target shopper searches and set custom bids.

❦ **Daily budget** – I put in $500 for the budget. Egad! $500? Don't worry, Amazon won't spend that much money. I set up a large budget because I want Amazon to continue sending out my ads without interruption. Even though my budget is set to $500, most days I'm only billed a few dollars. You are charged when a person clicks on your advertisement, not impressions. (Currently I am running 128 campaigns, and my highest ad spend for a single day was $48.00 over the past 30 days.)

❦ **Targeting** – Defaults to 'Manual,' but for this ad, I'll select 'Automatic targeting.'

Campaign bidding strategy ●

● **Dynamic bids - down only**
We'll lower your bids in real time when your ad may be less likely to convert to a sale. Any campaign created before April 22, 2019 used this setting.

○ **Dynamic bids - up and down**
We'll raise your bids (by a maximum of 100%) in real time when your ad may be more likely to convert to a sale, and lower your bids when less likely to convert to a sale.

○ **Fixed bids**
We'll use your exact bid and any manual adjustments you set, and won't change your bids based on likelihood of a sale.

˅ Adjust bids by placement (replaces Bid+) ●

❋ **Campaign bidding strategy** – I'll select 'Dynamic bids - down only' so I have more control of my cost per clicks.

Ad Format

● **Custom text ad**
Add custom text to your ad to give customers a glimpse of the book.

○ **Standard ad**
Choose this option to advertise your products without custom text.

❋ **Ad Format** – I've tried both types of ads and they've delivered the same results. Here's an example of both:

kindleunlimited

**Magical Makeover:
Paranormal Women's
Fiction (Mystical Midlife
in Maine Book 1)**
Brenda Trim
★★★★⯪ 757
Kindle Edition
$2.99

kindleunlimited

**A Book & Candle
Mystery (The Complete
Series: Books 1-7)**
Aubrey Harper
*Witches. Werewolves.
Vampires. Ghosts. And so
much more! Seven full-length
paranormal cozy mystery
novels in one volume!*
★★★★⯪ 804
Kindle Edition
$0.99

> ➤ ***Standard ad*** – The *Magical Makeover* example is a standard ad. If you select this, you won't be able to add any text to the ads, but you are able to add multiple products to your campaign. As you can see in the image below, I've added four different products.

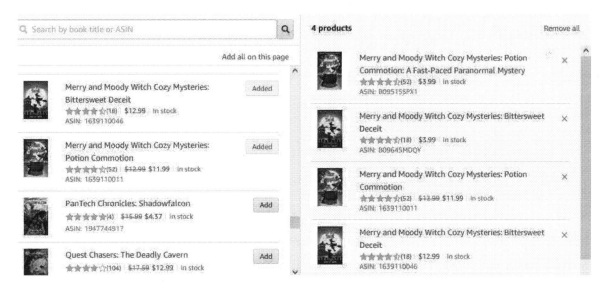

➤ ***Custom text ad*** – In the bundled example as you can see, there is additional ad text copy. I suggest trying both types to see which works best for you. If you're going to use the *Custom text ads*, add that information to your Campaign name. Since you'll only be able to use one product in that campaign, you can add whether it's an e-book, or a hardcopy in the campaign description. Notice in the image below that after I added an e-book, the other product's 'Add' button was grayed out.

❋ **Products** – In this campaign, I'll select *Custom text ads*. Therefore, I'll only be able to advertise one product.

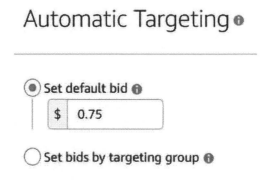

❋ **Set default bid** – The default bid for US campaigns is set to $0.75. When I first start out, since I'm trying to get into the 'Hot New Releases' in the first month, I set the bid between $0.50 to $1.00.

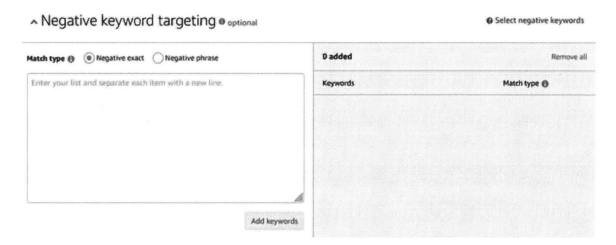

❀ **Negative keyword targeting** – For NKT, I tend to leave this alone if it's a new book or series. If not, I use my 'Negative Keywords' list that I've put together over the past several years and add them in.

❀ **Negative product targeting** – I leave this blank.

Creative

❀ **Creative** – Since I selected the *Custom text ads*, the option to add my ad copy shows up. The 'Custom text' box allows you to type in up to 150 characters.

❀ **Launch campaign!** Yay!

MANUAL TARGETING

When it comes to manual targeting, there are two different options. 'Keyword' or 'Product Targeting.' Let's start out with 'Keyword Targeting.'

Keyword Targeting

- ❀ **Campaign name** – I basically write the same text as in the Auto Targeting campaign, but without the word 'Auto'. If you want, you can even add the letters 'KW' for keywords: H2WXmasCozy KW 12/05/2021
- ❀ **Portfolio** – I would add it to the same portfolio I created for the Auto Targeting ad.
- ❀ **Start** – I use today's date.
- ❀ **End** – I leave this at 'No end date.'
- ❀ **Daily budget** – I type in $500 for the budget.

Targeting

◯ Automatic targeting
   Amazon will target keywords and products that are similar to the product in your ad.

◉ Manual targeting
   Choose keywords or products to target shopper searches and set custom bids.

- ❀ **Targeting** – This time, I select Manual targeting.
- ❀ **Campaign bidding strategy** – I select 'Dynamic bids - down only.'

Ad Format

◯ Custom text ad
   Add custom text to your ad to give customers a glimpse of the book.

◉ Standard ad
   Choose this option to advertise your products without custom text.

- ❀ **Ad Format** – I select Standard for now, so I'm able to add all my formats into one ad campaign.

❀ **Products** – I add the products that I'm going to advertise.

Targeting ⓘ

◉ **Keyword targeting**
Choose keywords to help your products appear in shopper searches.

◯ **Product targeting**
Choose specific products, categories, brands, or other product features to target your ads.

❀ **Targeting** – Select Keyword targeting.

❀ **Keyword targeting** – I never use the 'Suggested bid' option. I select the 'Default bid.' The 'Suggested bid' is usually much higher than needed, making your cost per click much more expensive. I tend to go lower in the bids for my keywords, maybe about 25 cents. Then, I'll make the decision whether to go up or down in ad spending depending on my clicks-to-buy. You can go through Amazon's Suggested Keywords. I always start with adding 'Broad' since this is basically the testing phase. After you've gone through their list, you can then click on 'Enter list' to add in your own keywords.

| Suggested ⓘ | **Enter list** | Upload file |

Bid ⓘ   Default bid ⌄ $ 0.25

Match type ⓘ   ☑ Broad   ☐ Phrase   ☐ Exact

> Enter your list and separate each item with a new line.

Add keywords

> ➤ You can use Publisher Rocket to find keywords through AMS Keyword Search.
> ➤ You can add in what you believe your target audience would search for to find your book.
> ➤ You can research your competitors' books on Amazon for keyword phrases in their book details.
> ➤ You can add in author names or book titles that are similar to your book.

❀ **Negative keyword targeting** – I leave this alone.

❀ Since I selected the *Standard ad* option, there is no ad copy text.

❀ **Launch campaign!**

Now let's create another manual targeting campaign with product targeting.

Product Targeting

❀ **Campaign name** – I write the same text as before, but I add in products: H2WXmasCozy Products 12/05/2021.

❀ **Portfolio** – I add it to the same portfolio I created for the Auto Targeting ad.

❀ **Start** – I use today's date.

❀ **End** – I leave it at 'No end date.'

❀ **Daily budget** – I enter $500 for the budget.

❀ **Targeting** – I select Manual targeting.

❀ **Campaign bidding strategy** – I select 'Dynamic bids - down only.'

❀ **Ad Format** – I'll select *Standard ad* again.

❀ **Products** – I add the products I'm advertising.

Targeting ●

○ Keyword targeting
 Choose keywords to help your products appear in shopper searches.

◉ Product targeting
 Choose specific products, categories, brands, or other product features to target your ads.

❀ **Targeting** – I select 'Product targeting.'

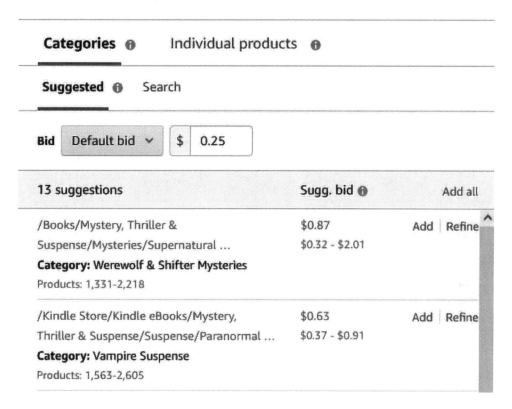

❀ **Product targeting** – I select the 'Default bid.' I'll start with 25 cents and go up or down from there as needed.

➤ I go through Amazon's suggested categories first. If there are none listed, I hit the 'Search' button, and type in 'mystery.'

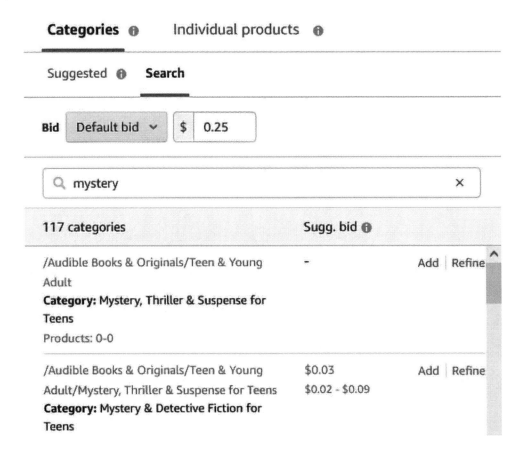

Make sure you read the entire category section. For example, the first one that shows up is */Audible Books & Originals/Teen & Young Adult*. I'm not advertising to Teen & Young Adults, nor do I have an audiobook, so I'll skip that one. If you did compile a list of categories in the previous section, you can find those on here. If you hit 'Refine,' it takes you to the following screen:

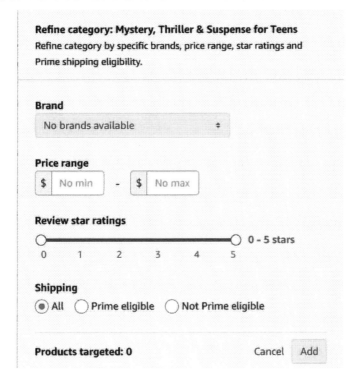

I tried using 'Refine' before, but I hardly got any impressions, so I skip that and just hit 'Add' to any relevant categories.

➤ I click on Individual products and add any suggestions that are relevant to my book.

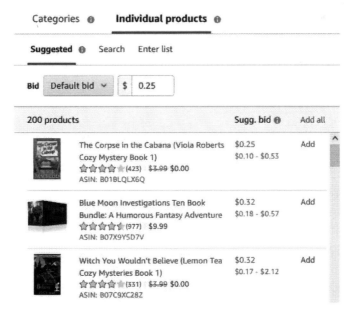

Then I head over to 'Search' and type in an author's name. For example, Mary Higgins Clark.

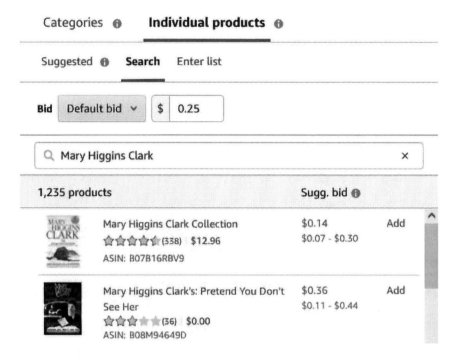

At this point, I add in any books I want to advertise against. However, if I've compiled a list of my competitors' books beforehand, I would choose 'Enter list.'

If you have Publisher Rocket, you can grab a list using AMS Keyword Search. 'Christmas Cozy' brings in a list of keywords and products. Here's a snapshot of the products:

I scrolled down for this image since the beginning of the list showed the keyword phrases, which we're not using in this ad. To complete this process, I would export the list, go through the products that are similar to my story, then head over to 'Enter List,' and paste in the ASINs.

❁ **Negative keyword targeting** – I leave this alone.

❁ I selected the *Standard ad,* so there is no ad copy text.

❁ Launch campaign!

OPTIMIZING CAMPAIGNS

Targeting

Amazon has created an amazing new tab called 'Targeting.' This new feature has saved me hours of work. I look at my numbers every few days, but don't really do much tweaking since the reported sales don't show up immediately, so I tend to see higher expenses in the beginning. If you need to look at your sales, you can go to your KDP account, hit 'Reports' at the very top, and compare the sales to your Advertising campaigns. FYI, if someone bought a paperback, it only shows up in sales when it ships, not when it was ordered. I've found in my reports where at times it has taken Amazon a month to ship a paperback after the customer bought it.

After a couple of weeks of advertising, I go to my advertising account, and click on the 'Targeting' menu selection, located at the top of the page.

Next, I navigate to 'Filter', which usually has 'Active status: Enabled' already entered into the 'Filter' field.

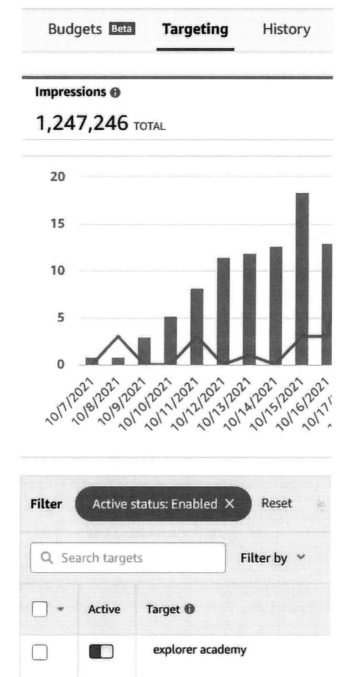

Then I go to 'Filter by' so I can apply more criteria:

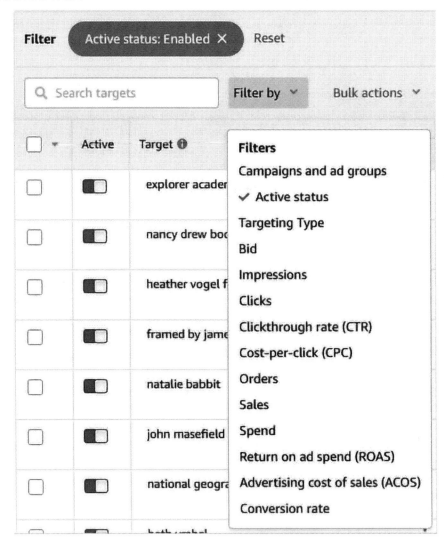

If I choose 'Impressions,' the following text box will show up.

In this case, I'll leave it as 'greater than.' However, they do have a few other options, which I show in the image below.

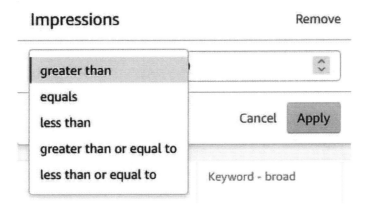

I'll explain why I choose 'greater than' in a moment, for now, I'll add in 1,000 impressions, then hit Apply.

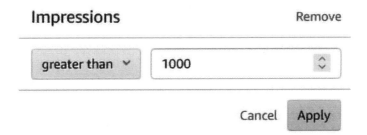

Here are the criteria I'm going to use:

❀ Impressions: greater than 1000

❀ Clicks: greater than 0

❀ CTR: less than 0.20%

❀ Orders: equals 0

Your filter section will end up looking like the image below.

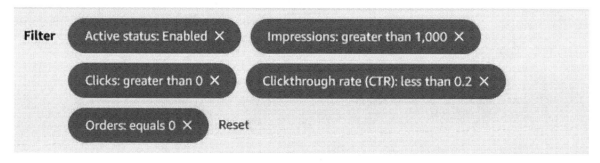

Next, go to 'Date range' on the far right, and make sure that it's set appropriately.

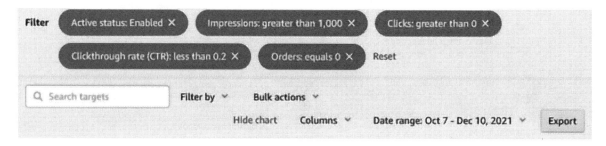

I like to use the 'Lifetime' option.

Today
Yesterday
Last 7 days
This week
Last week
Last 30 days
This month
Last month
Year to date
Lifetime

America/Los_Angeles

‹   **October 2021**   **November 2021**   **›**

Su	Mo	Tu	We	Th	Fr	Sa		Su	Mo	Tu	We	Th	Fr	Sa
					1	2			1	2	3	4	5	6
3	4	5	6	7	8	9		7	8	9	10	11	12	13
10	11	12	13	14	15	16		14	15	16	17	18	19	20
17	18	19	20	21	22	23		21	22	23	24	25	26	27
24	25	26	27	28	29	30		28	29	30				
31														

Cancel   Apply

Now for my explanation. I use these criteria since Amazon ads tend to be less effective if the click-through rate is lower than 0.20%. So, I would need a click for every 500 impressions. I search for impressions over 1000 since I don't want to pause a keyword or product that receives a click after 501 impressions. I would need the clicks to be higher than zero, so I get a CTR number to work with. And I choose 'Orders equals zero' so I get the worst keywords first.

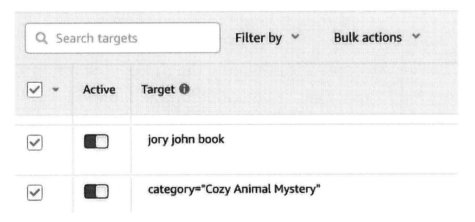

From the image above, I see that several of these 'Targets' need to be paused for having a CTR of 0.03% to 0.05%. If that comprises the entire list—instead of checking each target one by one—I click on the box on the left of 'Active'. That selects all the targets.

I then hit 'Bulk actions,' which shows me the following dropdown list.

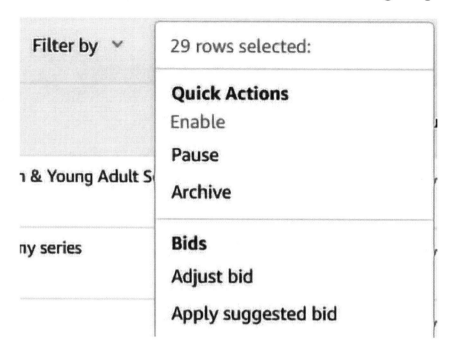

From here, I select 'Pause.'

Afterward, I would remove the 'Orders equals 0' criteria from my Filter list and see if there are any keywords that are still way below 0.20%. Even though it made a sale, it doesn't mean the keyword is relevant to my book.

I prefer to work with *orders* instead of *sales*. Here's why. Let's say that I ran a free book promotion. When readers download your e-book for free, your orders go up, and Sales would equal zero.

IMPORTANT Amazon doesn't show the *Pages Read* in this section. So, if you want to see if there were any Kindle Unlimited downloads, click the Ad Group link. It's located at the right of the following image.

When you click 'Ad group' It will open a new tab in your browser.

Sort your keywords by 'KENP read' on the far right to see which keywords are performing. You can cross-reference your results with the 'Targeting' section. Make sure you don't pause a keyword that was performing well with Kindle Unlimited readers.

Work with 'Targeting' at least once a week to make sure your ads are performing well.

Search Terms

Another amazing thing Amazon added to their advertising platform is a list of the customers' search terms. To find which queries they used, click on a campaign. In this example, I'll start with the Auto-Targeting Campaign:

Click on an Ad Group.

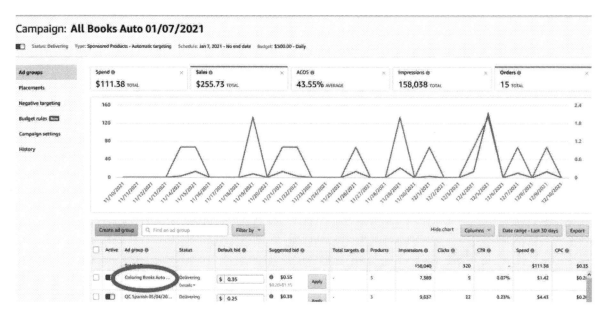

On the left-hand side, you'll see the 'Search terms' tab.

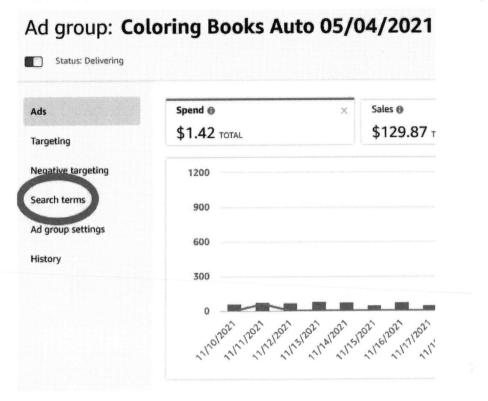

You'll notice on the far right that you have the following buttons: 'Columns,' 'Date range – Last 30 days,' and 'Export.' Go ahead and click on 'Date range – Last 30 days.'

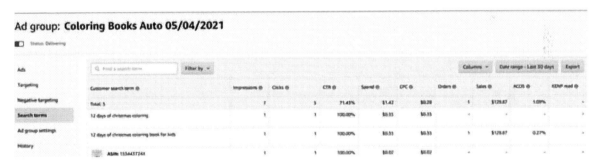

I wish you could go further back, but Amazon only allows you to see the past 65 days. Make sure you come back and check this out about once a month.

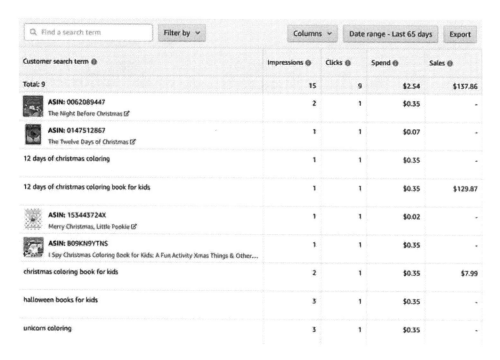

Select 'Last 65 days.' The following is an image of the customer's search terms.

Since this is in an Auto-Targeting Campaign, there are no buttons to easily add profitable keywords or negative keywords. However, you can export this table and add it to a spreadsheet or notepad to reference.

According to the previous example, the profitable keywords would be:

❄ 12 days of Christmas coloring book for kids

❄ Christmas coloring book for kids

The *products*—which are the ones with the book image and ASIN information—did not make a sale. However, if they did, then I would copy the ASIN number and paste it on my profitable list.

As for making a list of my negative keywords, nothing really pops up. The products I'm advertising are a range of themed-coloring books which include Christmas, Halloween, Unicorn, and so on. If there was a keyword or product that had 20 clicks and zero buys, then I would add that keyword or the product's ASIN to my negative list. Also, if I see any search terms that are irrelevant, I also add those to my negative list.

ADDING NEGATIVE KEYWORDS AND PRODUCTS

Here's how I add Negative Keywords and Products to my campaign. First I select the 'Negative targeting' button, on the left-hand side of the screen.

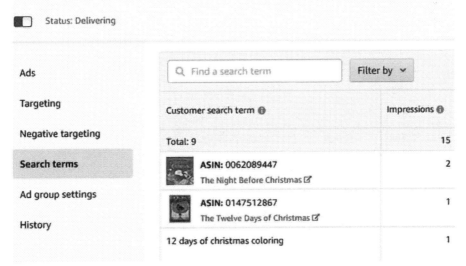

Once I click the 'Negative targeting,' the following is displayed:

Notice that there are two options. 'Negative keywords' and 'Negative products.' If I had a list of negative keywords, I would add the search terms. If I had 'Negative products' I would add the ASINs.

In the first example, let's say I have a negative keyword list. I would click the 'Add negative keywords' button. Which would display the following window:

I would paste my negative keywords list here. Amazon gives you the option to add a 'negative exact' or 'negative phrase.' I always start with 'negative exact.' Once this is done, I would select 'Add keywords.' They'll pop up on the right-hand side to the 'Added' section.

If some of the words you entered from your list weren't added, it's most likely you already have it as a negative keyword, or because it has some special character(s) in the text.

Now add in your negative phrases. Select 'Add keywords.' It'll pop up in your 'Added' list section, then hit 'Save.'

ADDING PROFITABLE KEYWORDS

Now let's move on to adding your *Profitable Keywords* and *Profitable Products* list. For these, you may want to create a new 'Manual Targeting Campaign' where it only advertises your book to profitable keywords and products. Let's start with the keywords.

Select 'Create Campaign,' and then name your campaign.

❀ **Campaign name** – H2WXmasCozy Profitable KW 12/05/2021.

❀ **Portfolio** – NF.

❀ **Start** – Today's date.

❀ **End** – No end date.

❀ **Daily budget** –$500.

❀ **Targeting** – Manual targeting.

❀ **Campaign bidding strategy** –Dynamic bids - down only.

❀ **Ad Format** – Standard ads (Up to you if you want custom).

❀ **Products** – All the formats of *How to Write and Market a Christmas Cozy Mystery*.

❀ **Targeting** – Keyword targeting.

❀ **Keyword targeting** – Select 'Enter list.'

➤ **Bid** – Select 'Default Bid.' Since these are profitable, I may go on the higher end for cost per click. I would most likely keep it above $0.50.

➤ **Match type** – I tend to select *Phrase* and *Exact* since I know these custom search terms were profitable. *Broad* is basically already in the Auto Targeting Campaign.

➤ **Profitable Keywords** - Paste your *Profitable Keywords* list in the box below and hit 'Add keywords.'

❀ **Negative keyword targeting** – Blank.

❀ **Launch campaign!**

Alright, now that that's out of the way, let's add the *Profitable Products*. To do this, repeat the exact same process, starting with 'Create Campaign.'

❀ **Campaign name** – H2WXmasCozy Profitable Products 12/05/2021.

❀ **Portfolio** – NF.

- ❀ **Start** – Today's date.
- ❀ **End** – No end date.
- ❀ **Daily budget** –$500.
- ❀ **Targeting** – Manual targeting.
- ❀ **Campaign bidding strategy** –Dynamic bids - down only.
- ❀ **Ad Format** – Standard ads (Up to you if you want custom).
- ❀ **Products** – All the formats of *How to Write and Market a Christmas Cozy Mystery*.
- ❀ **Targeting** – Product targeting.
- ❀ **Product targeting** – Select 'Individual products,' then hit 'Enter list.'
  - ➤ Bid – Select Default Bid. I would most likely keep it above $0.50.
  - ➤ Paste the profitable ASINs list in the text box and select 'Add keywords.'
- ❀ **Negative keyword targeting** – Blank.
- ❀ **Launch campaign!**

All these additional steps are necessary when you're working with the 'Auto-Targeting Campaign.' It's a lot more manual work since you cannot add keywords or products to an auto-targeting campaign.

Finally, it's time to find profitable and negative search terms in your 'Manual Targeting Campaigns.'

Let's start with the keywords. Click on your 'Manual Targeting – Keywords Campaign.' Select the Ad Group and go to 'Search Terms.'

Remember to head over to 'Date range' on the right-hand side to select 'Last 65 days.'

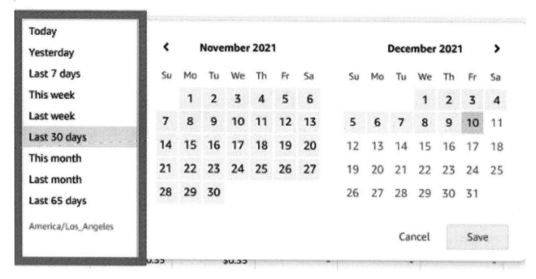

Once everything has been populated, you'll notice the 'Search Terms' section looks slightly different than the Auto-Targeting Campaign.

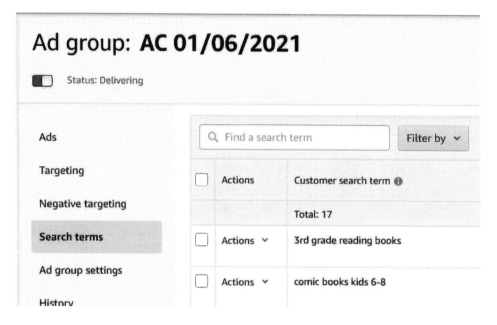

If you select a keyword, two buttons pop up: 'Add as keyword' and 'Add as negative keyword' as shown in the following image.

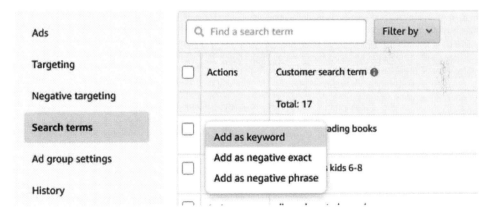

This window enables you to select multiple keywords and add them as new keywords or as negative keywords to your campaign. However, if you prefer to go keyword by keyword, you can use the 'Actions' dropdown to the left of the customer search term. To use this option, none of the keywords should be selected. Once you click on the 'Actions' dropdown menu, you'll see the following options:

If it's a profitable keyword, select 'Add as keyword.' If it's an irrelevant or costly keyword, then select 'Add as negative exact' and/or 'Add as negative phrase.'

Once you're done with this campaign, head on over to your 'Manual Targeting – Products Campaign.' Select your Ad Group and go to 'Search Terms.' You'll see the book images and ASINs in this section.

Everything is basically the same as the 'Manual Targeting – Keywords Campaign,' but the wording is a little different. For example, if you select the 'Actions' button on the left of a 'Matched product,' you'll see 'Add as product target' or 'Add as negative product.' See the following image.

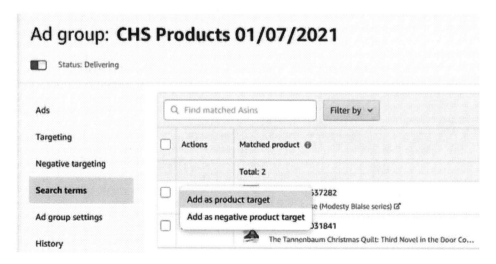

Same as when you select a product, you'll see the buttons with the same wording.

1 row selected:	Add as product target	Add as negative product target

	Actions	Matched product ⓘ
☐		
		Total: 2
☑	Actions ⌄	**ASIN: 0285637282** Modesty Blaise (Modesty Blaise series) ☑
☐	Actions ⌄	**ASIN: 1644031841** The Tannenbaum Christmas Quilt: Third Novel in the Door Co...

Go ahead and select the profitable products and hit 'Add as product target.' Then select the unprofitable or irrelevant ones and hit 'Add as negative product target.' Make sure to do this every month or two. Don't wait until the 65th day, or you'll lose the chance to find any important search terms or matched products.

FACEBOOK OR META (SNICKER)

If you want to run advertisements on Facebook or Meta (snicker, snicker) you'll need to set up a Facebook ads manager account: business.facebook.com/adsmanager/

Once you've set up your ads manager account, you can start creating ad campaigns.

business.facebook.com/adsmanager/manage/campaigns

Campaign

Creating your first ad campaign. Start by selecting the 'Create New Campaign' button.

Create New Campaign	Use Existing Campaign	✕

Choose a Campaign Objective
Learn More

Awareness	Consideration	Conversion
○ Brand awareness	○ Traffic	○ Conversions
○ Reach	○ Engagement	○ Catalog sales
	○ App installs	○ Store traffic
	○ Video views	
	○ Lead generation	
	○ Messages	

Cancel   Continue

You'll see a lot of choices such as traffic, engagement, lead generation messages. Currently, I only use three of the campaign choices.

Traffic – I use traffic to send customers directly to my Amazon link. There is a lot of controversy around using an Amazon affiliate link. I've been told by multiple sources that Amazon will cancel your affiliate account. So, I simply copy the URL and send people directly to the book that I am marketing.

NOTE A quick point of interest about the Amazon URL, the link for your book can at times be very long.

You don't need all that information—all you need is up to the product ID. So the shortened URL below, will work just as effectively as the long URL.

Lead Generation – I use lead generation when I'm working on building my mailing list.

Conversions – I use conversions if I'm sending people to my website and using Facebook pixels. (A Facebook pixel is a piece of code that you add to your website that allows you to measure the effectiveness of your advertising by understanding the actions people take on your website. Facebook uses this information to make sure the ads are shown to the correct target audience.)

I'm going to select Traffic.

Awareness	Consideration	Conversion
◯ Brand awareness	● Traffic	◯ Conversions
◯ Reach	◯ Engagement	◯ Catalog sales

Once I select Traffic, you'll see three options: 'Name this campaign,' 'Name this ad set,' 'Name this ad.' I usually use my book's initials and, depending on my targeting or what type of ads I'm using, I'll add a little extra information.

Traffic

Send people to a website, app, or Facebook event, or let them tap to call you. Learn more

Name your campaign · Optional   ⌃

📁 **Campaign**
Includes the campaign objective and budget optimization.

> Name this campaign

🔳 **Ad set**
Determines your audience, placements, schedule and spending.

Create ad set ▼	Name this ad set

🗔 **Ad**
Contains all ad creative settings.

Create ad ▼	Name this ad

Cancel   Continue

Once you hit 'Continue,' scroll down and you'll see 'Campaign Budget Optimization.' If you're going to run more than one ad group, this is an option. If you're looking to test each ad group, like an A/B Split Test, keep this *Off* and Facebook should spend an equal amount of money for each ad group.

Traffic

Send people to a website, app, or Facebook event, or let them tap to call you. Learn more

Show more options ▾

A/B Test   Create A/B Test 🔘

Try different images, ad text, audiences, and more to see which one performs best. Learn more

Campaign Budget Optimization   Off 🔘
Campaign budget optimization will distribute your budget across ad sets to get more results depending on your delivery optimization choices and bid strategy. You can control spending on each ad set. Learn more

If you selected *On*, type in the amount of your initial budget. I suggest starting at $5 and working up monetary increments slowly, depending on your ad performance. Once this is done, press 'Next' to start working on the ad set.

Ad Set

You'll see 'Dynamic Creative' is set to *Off*. I would suggest turning that *On* so you can test different texts/images/videos/buttons and let Facebook perform at its best.

Dynamic Creative   Off ●

Provide creative elements, such as images and headlines, and we'll automatically generate combinations optimized for your audience. Variations may include different formats or templates based on one or more elements. Learn More

If you decided to leave 'Campaign Budget Optimization' *Off*, you'll need to add your budget in this Ad Set section.

For Audiences, I try to hit a target group of about 1,000,000. You don't want to go too much higher than a million or too much lower. Facebook provides a handy little graphic to let you know if your audience is too specific or too broad.

Audience Definition

Your audience selection is fairly broad.

Specific   Broad

Estimated audience size: 866,500 - 1,000,000 ●

Estimates may vary significantly over time based on your targeting selections and available data.

The Audience creation section enables you to define who sees your ads. It's broken up into custom/existing audiences, location, age, gender, detailed targeting and languages. Developing the correct audience is exceptionally important. If you're writing cozy mysteries, you don't want to target 18-year-old men. At least, I don't think you do.

Create New Audience   Use Saved Audience ▾

Custom Audiences   Create new ▾

> 🔍 Search existing audiences

Exclude

Locations

Location:
- United States

Age

18 - 65+

Gender

All genders

Detailed Targeting

All demographics, interests and behaviors

Languages

All languages

Show more options ▾

Save This Audience

❄ **LOCATION** You may prefer to use one ad group per country, or one audience interest per ad group, etc. In this example, I'm adding the following countries together into one ad group: Australia,

Canada, United Kingdom, United States. To do this, hover over Location, click Edit, and add them in.

❧ **AGE** Since you are working on cozy mysteries, I would suggest starting at 35 years old at the low end. Later on, I'll teach you which age group is least expensive.

❧ **GENDER** This depends on your book. If I have a witch cozy mystery for example, I would select *female*. However, if I have a male protagonist, I would select both *male* and *female*.

❧ **DETAILED TARGETING** This is where I do lots of testing. There are times where I choose only one 'Interest' per ad group. Other times, I'll add in several interest groups to see which performs the best.

➤ You can add in the genre
➤ You can add in big-time authors
➤ You can even add in holidays

After I specify which 'Interest,' I look at the target group and make sure I'm way over 1,000,000. If not, I'll add another interest that's similar to what I just added. Let's say I select *Cozy mystery*, my audience size would be the following:

Audience Definition

Your audience selection is fairly broad.

Specific   Broad

Estimated audience size: 1,300,000 - 1,500,000 ⓘ

〰 Estimates may vary significantly over time based on your targeting selections and available data.

Once I'm at an acceptable target group size, I'll click the 'Narrow Audience' button.

Detailed Targeting

Include people who match ❶

Interests > Additional Interests
Cozy mystery

Q Add demographics, interests or behaviors   Suggestions Browse

Exclude	Narrow Audience

Once I click that selection, the following text box will pop up:

and must also match ❶   ✕

Q Add demographics, interests or behaviors   Suggestions Browse

I usually add the following Interests: *Amazon Kindle*, *Kindle* and *Paperback*. I do this to let Facebook know that I want my audience to be interested in cozy mysteries *and* Kindle and Paperback. If you want it to be one *or* the other, then add it right under *Cozy mystery*.

If the audience size is too small, for example, maybe 500,000, then I would also add *Engaged Shoppers* in the 'include people who match' section.

If the audience is much larger than 1,000,000, I'd select 'Narrow Further' and add *Engaged Shoppers*.

❀ **DETAILED TARGETING EXPANSION** I leave this alone until my 'Frequency' number in the ads reporting is over 2, which means that each targeted person has seen my ad twice.

❀ **LANGUAGES** I choose *English (UK)* and *English (US)*.

Once you've completed filling in this information, click 'Save the Audience,' in case you want to be able to access it later.

For 'Placements,' I leave it at Automatic.

Placements   Learn more

⦿ **Automatic placements (recommended)**
Use automatic placements to maximize your budget and help show your ads to more people. Facebook's delivery system will allocate your ad set's budget across multiple placements based on where they're likely to perform best.

○ **Manual placements**
Manually choose the places to show your ad. The more placements you select, the more opportunities you'll have to reach your target audience and achieve your business goals.

Show more options ▾

I used to select 'Facebook News Feed' under Manual, but I've seen better results with Facebook's Automatic Placements. Facebook has spent millions of dollars on their algorithm, so I trust them to know what they are doing when delivering ads to the correct audience.

Everything else I leave alone and hit 'Next.'

Ad

Once you click 'Next,' you'll be taken to the following screen. It's a busy screen, don't be intimidated!

Ad name

New Traffic Ad   Create template

Identity

Facebook Page

Twisted Key Publishing ▼

Instagram account ❶

🏳 Use selected Page ▼ or [Connect account]

Ad setup

Create ad ▼

⬤ **Dynamic formats and creative**
Automatically optimize your ad's format, creative and
destination for each person when you use a catalog.
This lets you personalize your ads on a larger scale.
See how

Format
Choose how you'd like to structure your ad.

⦿ Single image or video
One image or video, or a slideshow with multiple images

◯ Carousel
2 or more scrollable images or videos

◯ Collection
Group of items that opens into a fullscreen mobile experience

❀ **IDENTITY** Select the Facebook Page you want to run your ads
from. I've heard of people getting better results if your Page is
generic. For example, "Witch Cozy Mystery Book Fans." However,
I believe running it through your Author Facebook Page can make

it more personal for the audience and therefore can be just as, if not more effective.

❦ **AD CREATIVE** For Dynamic Creative ads, you can select up to 10 images or videos.

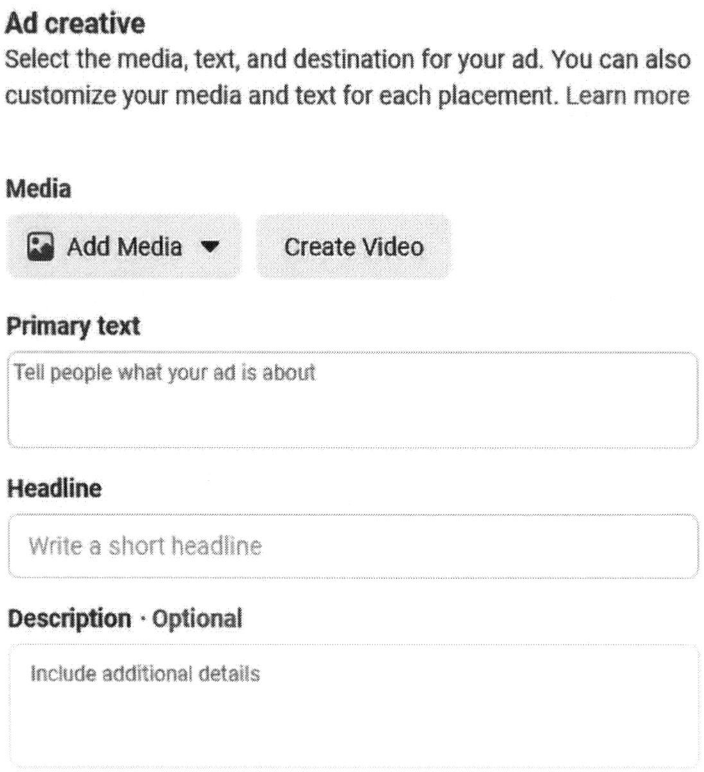

Ad creative

Select the media, text, and destination for your ad. You can also customize your media and text for each placement. Learn more

Media

[🖼 Add Media ▼]   [Create Video]

Primary text

Tell people what your ad is about

Headline

Write a short headline

Description · Optional

Include additional details

❦ You can add your ads by clicking on 'Add Media.' I've tried the following types of ads:

> ➤ Images with 3D mockups of the books alone, no background
> ➤ Images with text, background and 3D mockups of the books
> ➤ Shutterstock illustrated images alone (no book cover, no text)

Interestingly, the top five best-performing ads were the generic Shutterstock images without any other elements added. The first two ads in the following image are pictures from Shutterstock.

Believe it or not, the last ad, a 3D-mock up cover with text performed the worst.

I would experiment to see what works best for your genre and your audience. If you use Dynamic Creative, Facebook will decide which ads are performing the best and your CPC will be lower.

Once you add in your media, there's an option to optimize. If your image or video is not 1080 x 1080, but horizontal instead, make sure this isn't checked off. Facebook will cut your horizontal images or videos to a 1080 x 1080 square if you choose to optimize.

❋ **PRIMARY TEXT** Type in your sales pitch, then hit + Add Options to add another sales pitch.

Primary text   1 of 5

Tell people what your ad is about

⊕ Add options

Facebook allows five different ad texts. Try using them all to see what works best for your audience and genre. Ideas for ad texts are:

1) Sales/Promotion.

2) Review(s) – if it's a 5-star review, add the five-star icons for social proof. You don't have to include the entire review. You just need to include a snippet followed by an ellipsis.

3) Blurb.

4) An excerpt from your book.

5) Other books or authors that are similar to yours.

❦ **HEADLINE** I type my headlines in capital letters. Make sure, when you look at the previews, that the Headline text is completely visible. If it's too long (too many characters), Facebook hides the ending of it. **Ideas for your headlines:**

1) Mention your genre.

2) Have you received a review where they said it's hard to put your book down? Or that your book is amazing? Mention that.

3) Mention Sales/Promotion.

4) Is it a bestseller? Mention that in another Headline.

5) Use different terms used in the same genre. For example: cozy mystery, whodunit, murder mystery, etc.

❦ **DESCRIPTION** Keep this short, or it can be hidden because of the Call-to-Action button. Ideas for this can be:

1) Mention any of the Headline texts

2) If the button sends them to a certain website (Amazon or your website), let them know

3) Type in the hook (sales pitch)

Let's move on to the next section. What action do you want to take place?

Destination

● 🔗 Website

○ 🔲 Facebook Event

○ 📞 Phone call

Website URL

http://www.example.com/page

Enter the website URL field for your ad.

Build a URL parameter

Display link · Optional

Enter the link you want to show on your ad

Call Extension

☐ Show call extension on your website

Call to Action ⓘ

Learn more ▼

❀ **WEBSITE URL** The website URL field gives you a lot of options. You can send them directly to your Amazon sales page for your book. You can send them to your website. I like to send readers directly to my website for a couple reasons. First, it's *all* my content. When you send someone to Amazon, it's easy to lose them because they begin looking at everything else on Amazon. If I send them to my website, I control their environment, which means they'll see all of my books and they may even join my newsletter. If you're targeting several countries in your campaign, I would recommend signing up to use Books2read.com services. This website creates a link for your book that will redirect Amazon buyers to their country.

❧ **CALL TO ACTION** – Amazon gives you a lot of call-to-action prompts that you can offer to your potential customers. I usually select 'Learn More' and 'Shop Now.'

Once you've completed all these steps, press the 'Publish' button. If your ads seem to be underperforming, give them a little time. Facebook has what it calls a learning process. It usually takes Facebook seven days to learn your audience. So, wait at least a week before you begin tweaking your ads.

OPTIMIZING CAMPAIGNS

In one of my campaigns, I tested the following for my witch cozy mystery (the protagonist has a cat familiar):

Ad group 1: Cats / Fantasy

Gender:
Female

Language:
English (US)

People Who Match:
Interests: Kitty, Cat food, Cat Lovers, Kitty Cats or Black cat

And Must Also Match:
Interests: Fantasy world, Paranormal, fantasy books, Magic (paranormal) or Spell (paranormal)

And Must Also Match:
Interests: Amazon Kindle, Kindle or Paperback, Behaviors: Engaged Shoppers

Edit

Ad group 2: Castle / Fantasy

Gender:

Female

Language:

English (US)

People Who Match:

Interests: Castle (TV series)

And Must Also Match:

Interests: Fantasy world, Paranormal, fantasy books, Magic (paranormal) or Spell (paranormal)

And Must Also Match:

Interests: Amazon Kindle, Kindle or Paperback, Behaviors: Engaged Shoppers

Edit

Ad group 3: Murder Mysteries / Fantasy

Gender:

Female

Language:

English (US)

People Who Match:

Interests: Murder Mysteries, Kitty, Tana French, Clue (film), sherlock holmes, Cozy mystery, Hercule Poirot, Maureen Johnson, Agatha Christie's Marple, Murder on the Orient Express, Cold Case, Agatha Christie, Murder, She Wrote, Kitty Cats, Mary Higgins Clark, Agatha Christie's Poirot, Miss Marple or Kyra Davis

And Must Also Match:

Interests: Fantasy world, Paranormal, fantasy books, Magic (paranormal) or Spell (paranormal)

And Must Also Match:

Interests: Amazon Kindle, Kindle or Paperback, Behaviors: Engaged Shoppers

Edit

Ad group 4: Cozy Mystery

Gender:
Female

Language:
English (UK) or English (US)

People Who Match:
Interests: Cozy mystery

And Must Also Match:
Behaviors: Engaged Shoppers

Edit

After a week, my CPC (Cost Per Click) and CTR (Click Through Rate) were the following:

AD GROUPS	CPC	CTR
Ad group 1: Cats / Fantasy	$0.43	3.24%
Ad group 2: Castle / Fantasy	$0.58	2.37%
Ad group 3: Murder Mysteries / Fantasy	$0.38	3.36%
Ad group 4: Cozy Mystery	$0.22	6.83%

It makes sense that Cozy Mystery has the lowest CPC and the highest CTR. I wanted to run a test by adding "Fantasy" in Narrow Audience to "Ad group 4: Cozy Mystery", however the audience was incredibly small, even with all four countries.

Another thing I found interesting was that the Interest group for Castle was expensive because of the age group. For ages 35-44, the CPC was $0.66, whereas ages 45-54, the CPC was $0.54.

I found this information by clicking on the Campaign, and when I hovered over the 'Ad group 2: Castle / Fantasy,' it shows me the links: View Charts | Edit | Duplicate

I selected View Charts, and when I scrolled down, it shows the demographics.

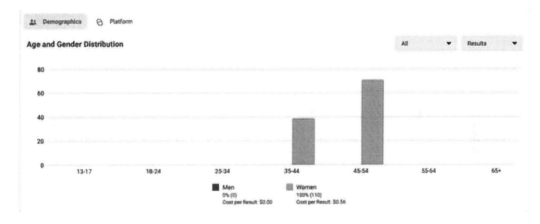

To change the dates you'd like to analyze, you'll need to update them on the top right-hand corner.

Under 'Age and Gender Distribution,' hover over the bars, and it'll give you more information on the CPC for each age group. If I look at the first graph and select the 'Per Link Click,' you'll notice how my ad started at a high CPC and then dropped quite a bit as Facebook learned how to serve my ads more effectively.

If I change my dates from October 17-19, it displays the following graph:

The CPC has dropped tremendously but the CTR increased by more than double. When I checked the age groups, they were both at 13

cents per click. Therefore, there was no need to change the age group for that ad set anymore. It's a CPC I'm completely comfortable with.

To nail down your audiences, you'll need to start by testing the audiences/ads. If you're going to hit Interest groups with very large audiences, it would be best to hit them in separate ad groups. While studying the results of this campaign, I learned that, depending on the 'Interest,' you may end up paying more per click, and not knowing which 'Interest' is expensive.

The biggest problem with Facebook is that you cannot see how much money you've made in book sales. You're only able to work with impressions, clicks, comments, etc. Luckily, when people engage with your ad, some of them say 'I just bought the book!' But that's about it. One thing you can do is compare your Facebook reporting with your KDP Sales Reporting and see if there's a bump in sales that's consistent with the timing and distribution of your new ad.

Finding the Best-Performing Campaign

Once you've found the best-performing audience and ad, you'll want to create a new Campaign without the Dynamic Creative. You can find the best performing audience by looking at the Ad sets section in your ads manager:

Ad Set Name	Results	Reach	Impressions	Cost per Result	Amount Spent
MM KU - Murder Mysteries / Fantasy View Charts Edit Duplicate	327 Link Clicks	6,506	11,537	$0.27 Per Link Click	$86.72
MM KU - Castle Fantasy	147 Link Clicks	4,725	8,070	$0.46 Per Link Click	$67.71
MM KU - Cats / Fantasy	235 Link Clicks	4,787	8,691	$0.33 Per Link Click	$77.16
MM KU Cozy Mystery	1,014 Link Clicks	8,013	21,926	$0.19 Per Link Click	$190.72
> Results from 4 ad sets ❶	1,723 Link Clicks	22,839 People	50,224 Total	$0.25 Per Link Click	$422.31 Total Spent

'MM KU Cozy Mystery' will be the ad set for my new campaign. When I click on that ad set, it will show me a single ad. To see *all* the ads in that ad set, I'll click 'Breakdown' on the right-hand side, navigate to 'Dynamic Creative Element' and go through that list.

❀ Image, Video Slideshow

❀ Text

❀ Headline

❀ Description

❀ Call To Action

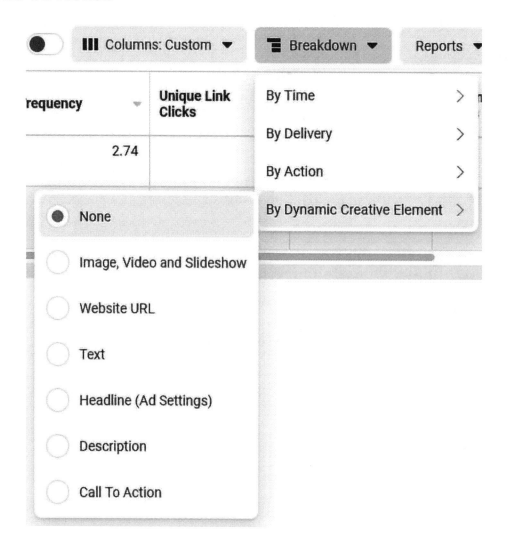

Let's start with 'Image, Video and Slideshow.' I like to look at the CTR (Click-through Rate) and Cost per Result. Even though the first image that shows up has a CTR of 8.06%, the Cost per Result is $0.24, so I would choose the second image on that list.

Ad Name	Results	Reach	Impressions	Cost per Result	CTR (All) ↓
MM KU - Can't Put Down	1,014 Link Clicks	8,013	21,926	$0.19 Per Link Click	6.40%
Image "shutterstock_1254693673.jpg_105_105_	23	356	422	$0.24	8.06%
Image "shutterstock_1507697876.jpg_105 (049_	323	2,681	5,696	$0.16	7.65%
Image "shutterstock_1537173029.jpg_105 (5f2_	54	833	1,072	$0.31	7.65%
Image "shutterstock_1027266772.jpg_105_105_	132	1,471	2,715	$0.17	6.85%
Image "shutterstock_1403947541.jpg_105 (ed7_	467	5,022	11,444	$0.19	5.64%
Image "shutterstock_1182682507.jpg_105 (0f4_	9	182	193	$0.22	5.18%
Image "untitled_105 (5ee4ac5867aa7a82c6791_	2	63	92	$0.31	3.26%
Image "untitled_105 (1e8d7acb43e523f773756_	2	82	97	$0.26	3.09%
Image "Potion Commotion 3d-mock up.png_10_	2	150	195	$0.63	2.05%
> Results from 1 ad ❶	1,014 Link Clicks	8,013 People	21,926 Total	$0.19 Per Link Click	6.40% Per Impressions

Next, I'll select 'Breakdown' again, choose 'Text' and analyze those results. I'll repeat the process for the remaining 'Dynamic Creative Elements.'

If CTR isn't showing up in the report, click on 'Column,' then hit 'Customize Columns.' You can add in the CTR from there, and any other metrics you'd like to analyze.

		Maximum: Nov 4, 2018 – Dec 4, 2021 ▾

ted ✕   ▣ **Ads for 1 Ad set**

● ◯   **III Columns: Custom ▾**   **≣ Breakdown: Image, Video and Slideshow ▾**   **Reports ▾**

	Unique Link Clicks ▾	Link Clicks ▾	Landing Page Views ▾
◯ Performance (Default)			
◯ Setup			
◯ Delivery	589	1,014	–
◯ Engagement			
◯ Video Engagement	–	23	–
◯ App Engagement	–	323	–
◯ Carousel Engagement	–	54	–
◯ Performance and Clicks	–	132	–
◯ Cross-Device	–	467	–
◯ Offline Conversions	–	9	–
◯ Targeting and Creative	–	2	–
◯ Bidding and Optimization			
◯ Messaging Engagement	–	2	–
◯ Digital Circular	–	2	–
● Custom Save	**589** Total	**1,014** Total	**–** Total
Customize Columns...			
Set as Default			

This information gives me everything I need to create my brand-new campaign. It's hard to catch people's attention, they're bombarded with ads and information constantly. So if you already have ads that are performing well, and they have a lot of comments, likes, and shares, don't start over from scratch! Make a couple changes and keep all of that incredible history and data that you've built up. Facebook will use that wealth of information to better distribute your ad to the right audience.

It can take months to have hundreds of comments, depending on your budget. If you make minor changes to reach a new audience but leave the rest of the ad alone, they'll see all that glorious social proof (hundreds of comments and shares) posted beneath your ads, and potential customers will be more likely to take interest in what you're offering. Sounds great, right?

I know that Amazon and Facebook advertising sounds daunting, and at first, it will be. The good thing is, we've created a Facebook group to help authors navigate through the craziness.

To learn more about the Cozy Mystery Facebook group, be sure to visit our resources webpage: christmascozymystery.com/resources.

As a way of saying thanks, our team has created a robust resource page filled with guides, charts, websites and software products to help you along your journey.

THANK YOU FOR READING

I am humbled that you purchased this book. Even though I struggled for hundreds of hours over the past few months writing it, I feel like I've produced a resource that will help people discover and fulfill their dreams of writing.

I constantly tell my daughter to live life to its fullest, but make sure to give back something of equal value. I truly hope that this simple book reaches a few hearts, and hope that it guides your fingers to pencil and paper or to a keyboard, where you'll one day share your story with us.

Thank you so much for reading *How to Write and Market a Christmas Cozy Mystery*. If you would, please take a moment and leave a review. Reviews are incredibly important to us, and we read each and every one. Thank you again!

Merry Christmas,
Thomas and Grace Lockhaven

Made in United States
Orlando, FL
23 September 2024

51837297R00146